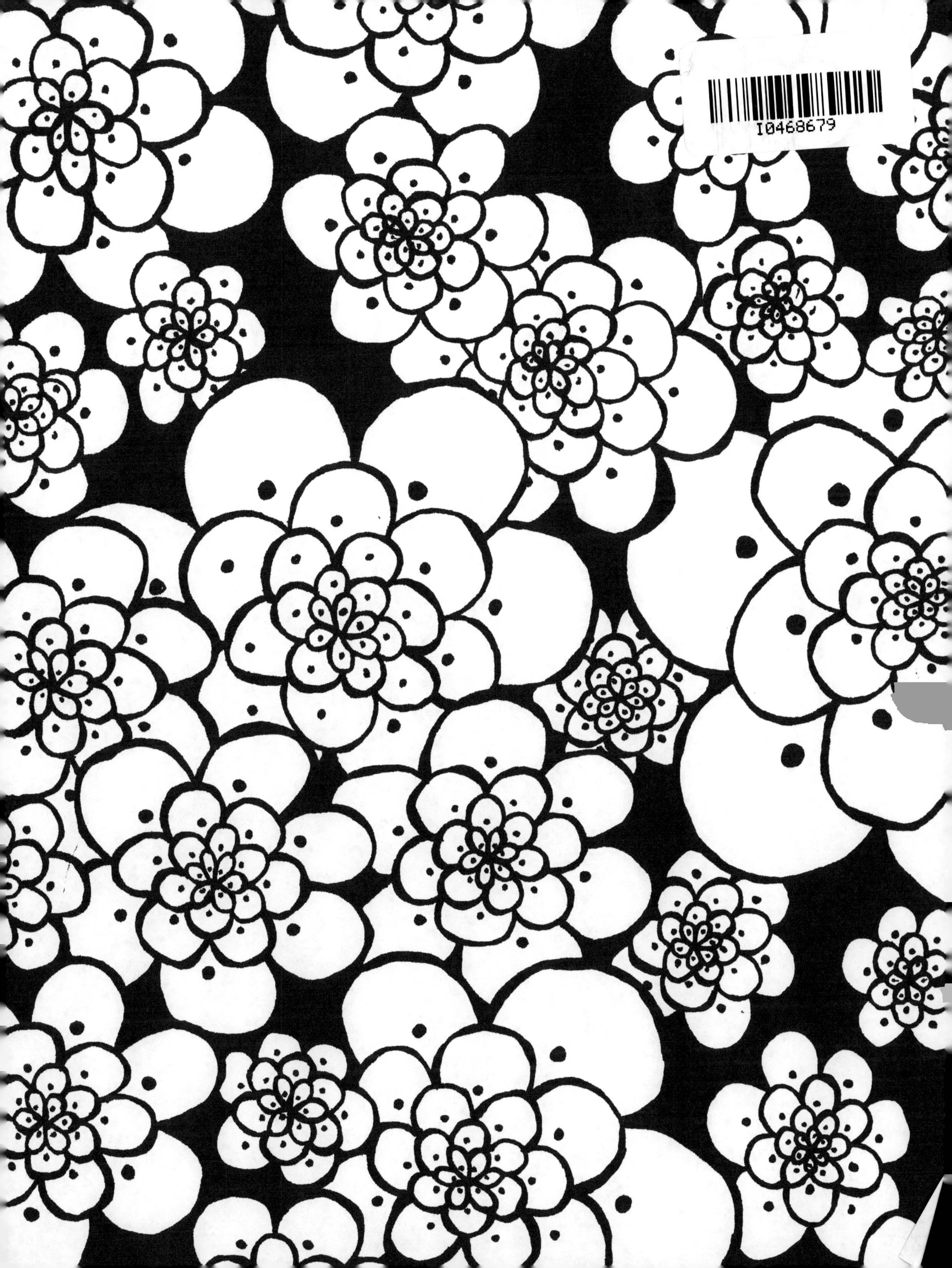

I0468679

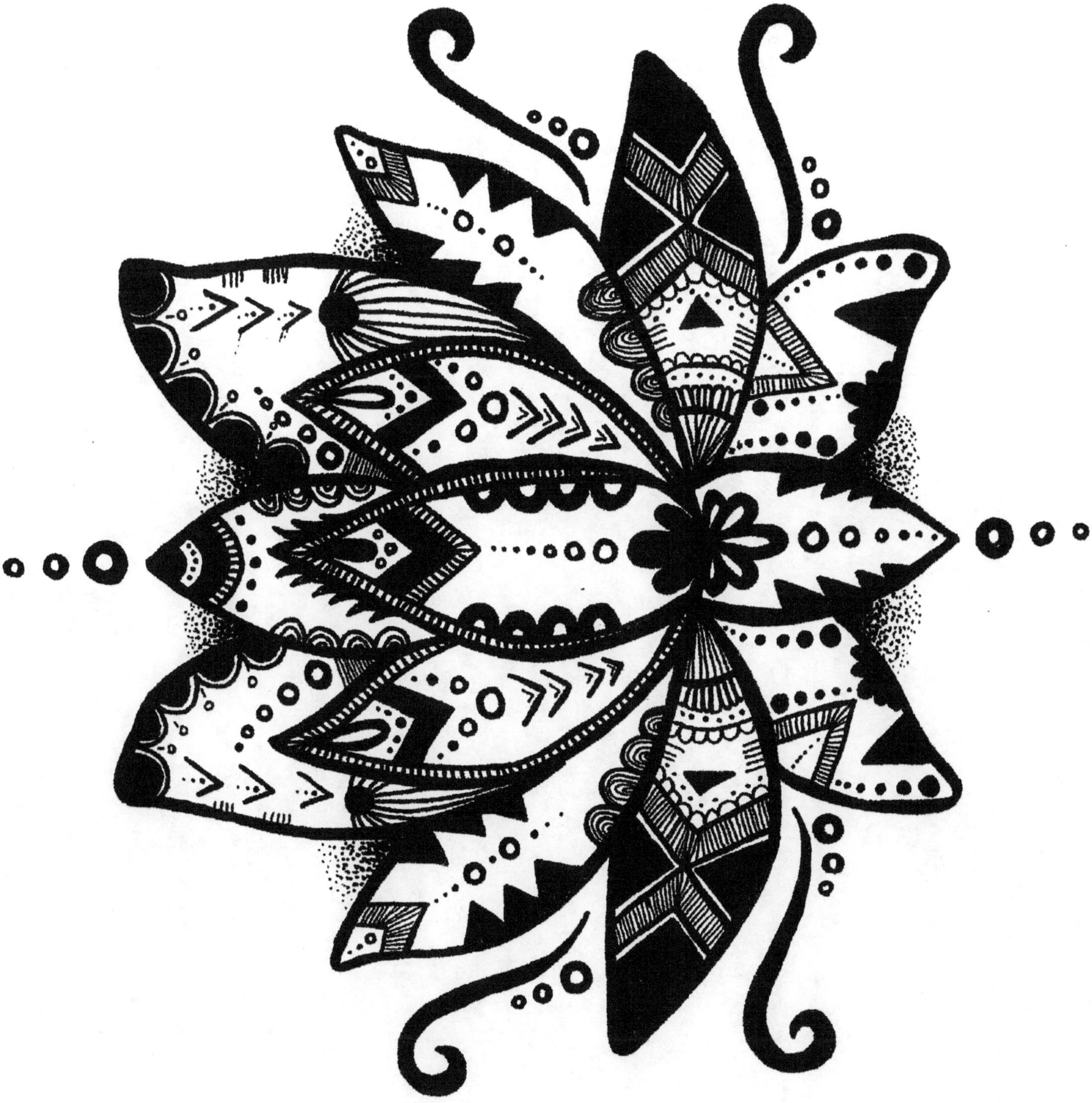

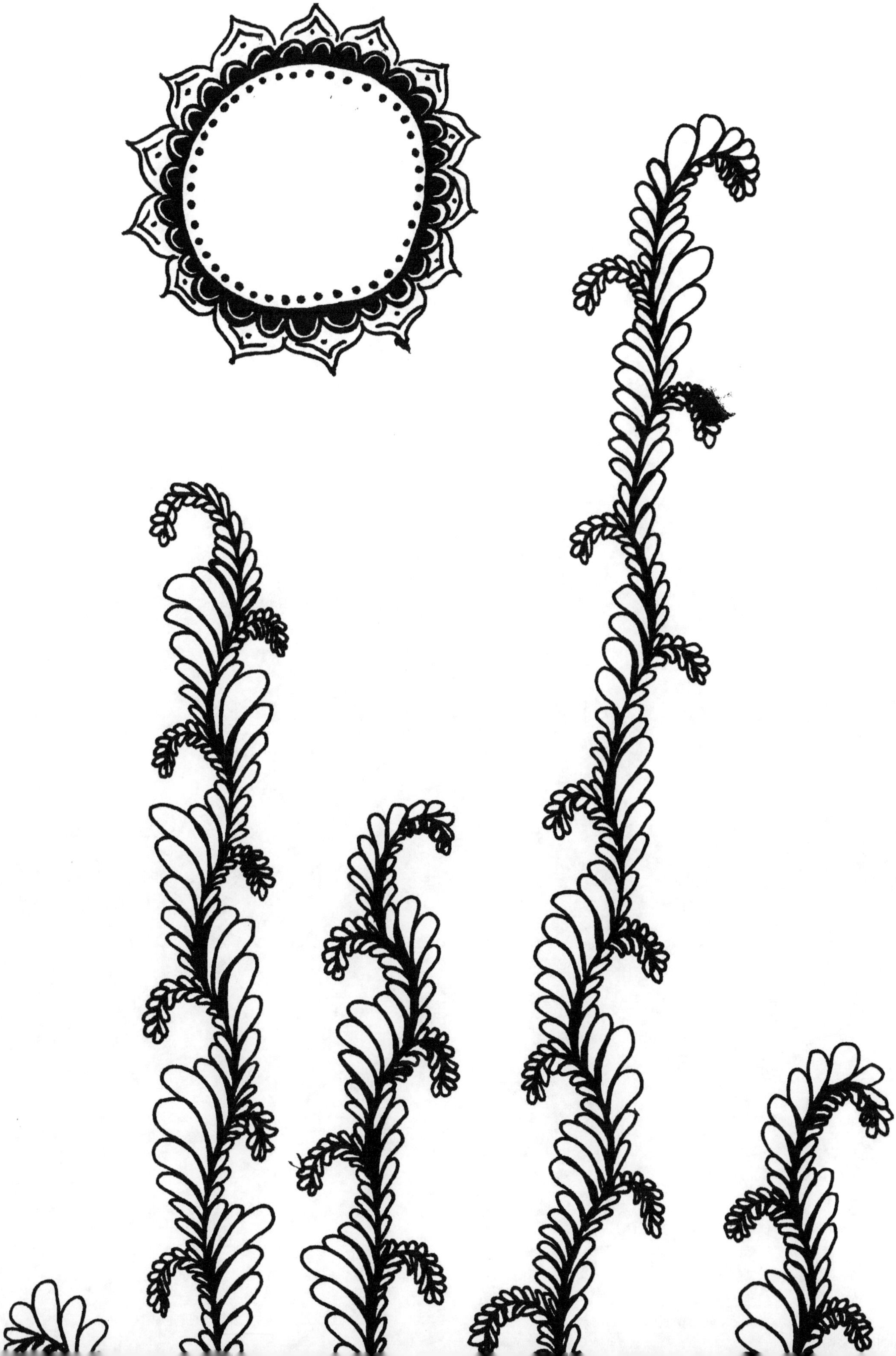

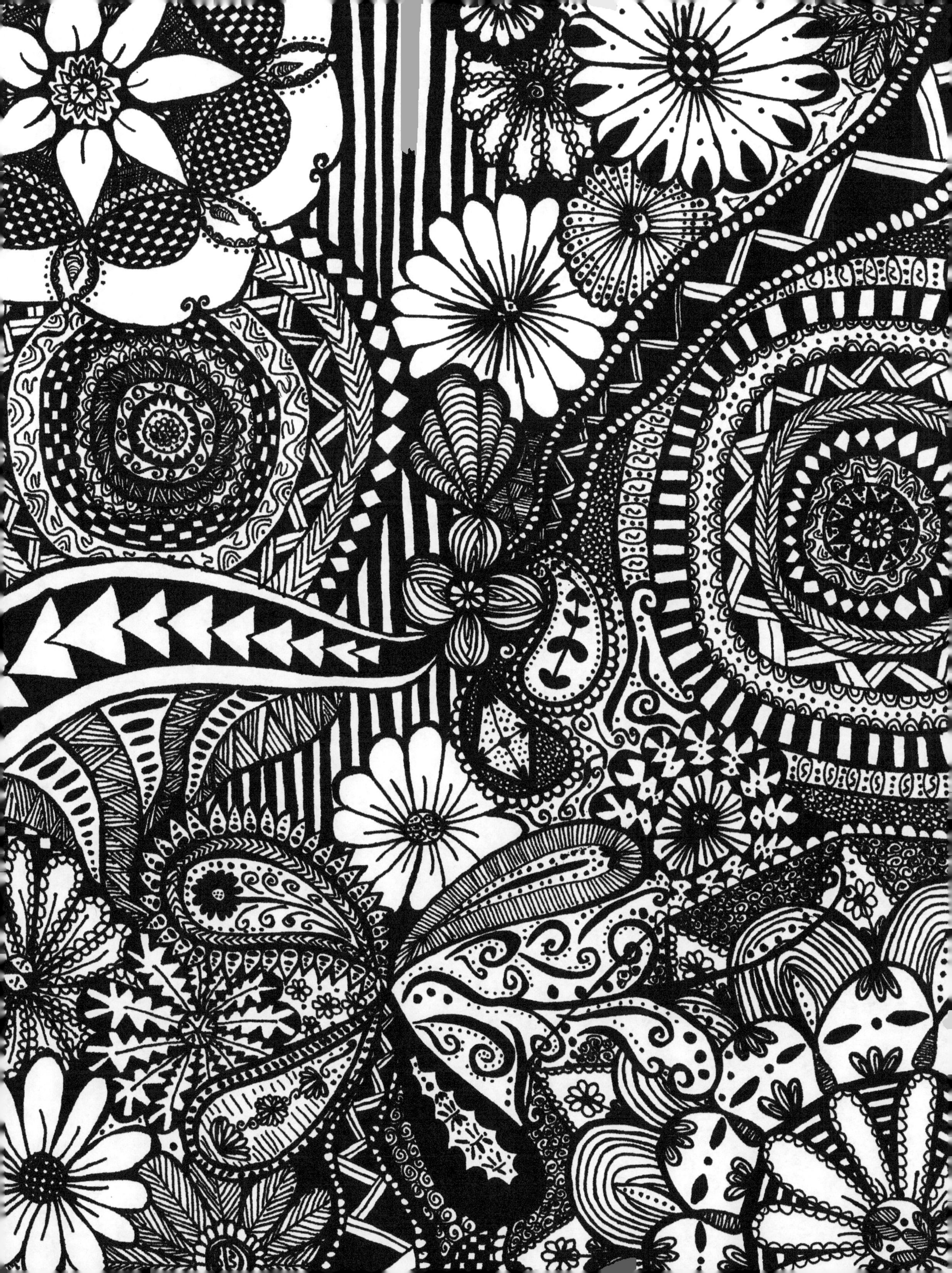

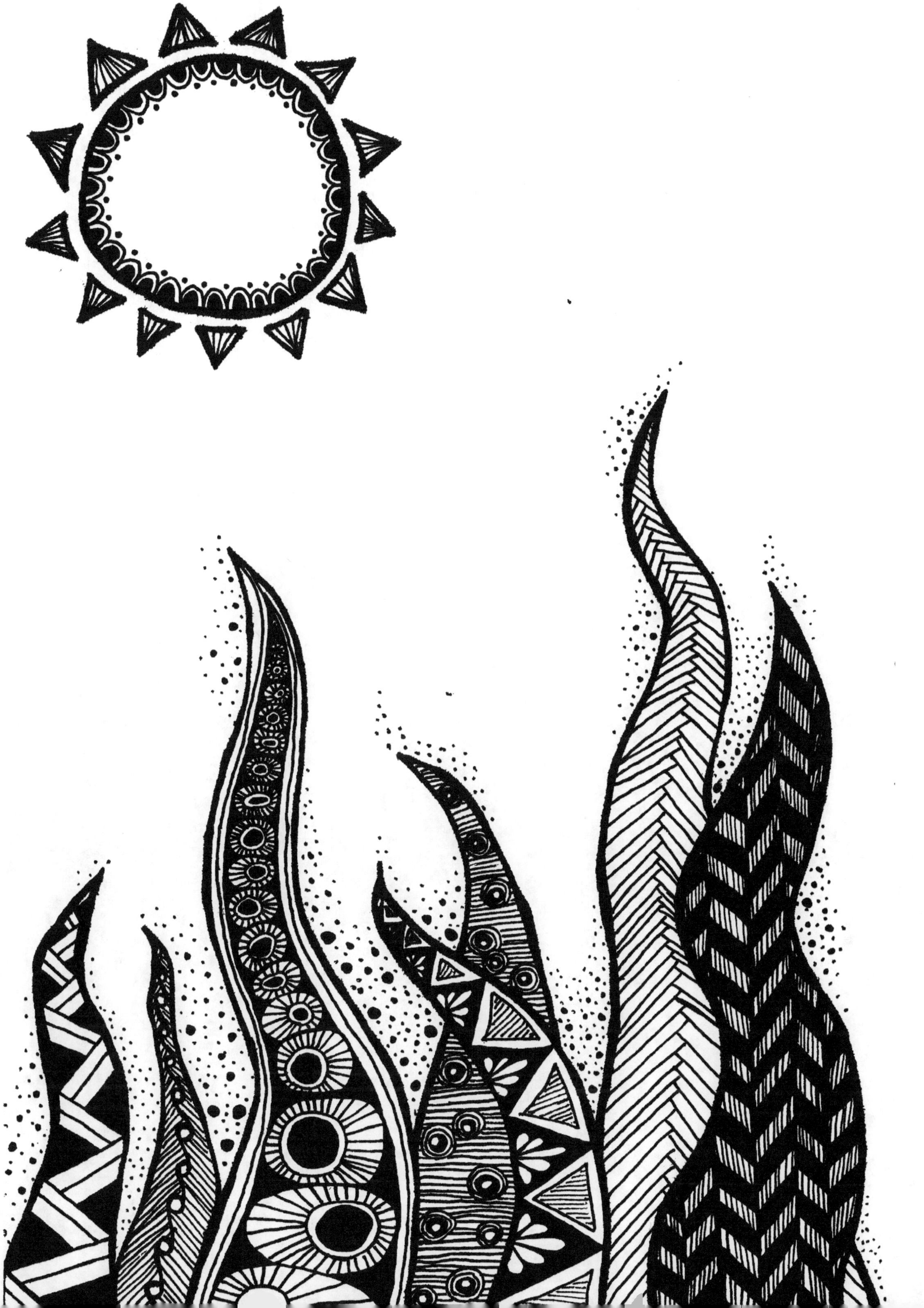

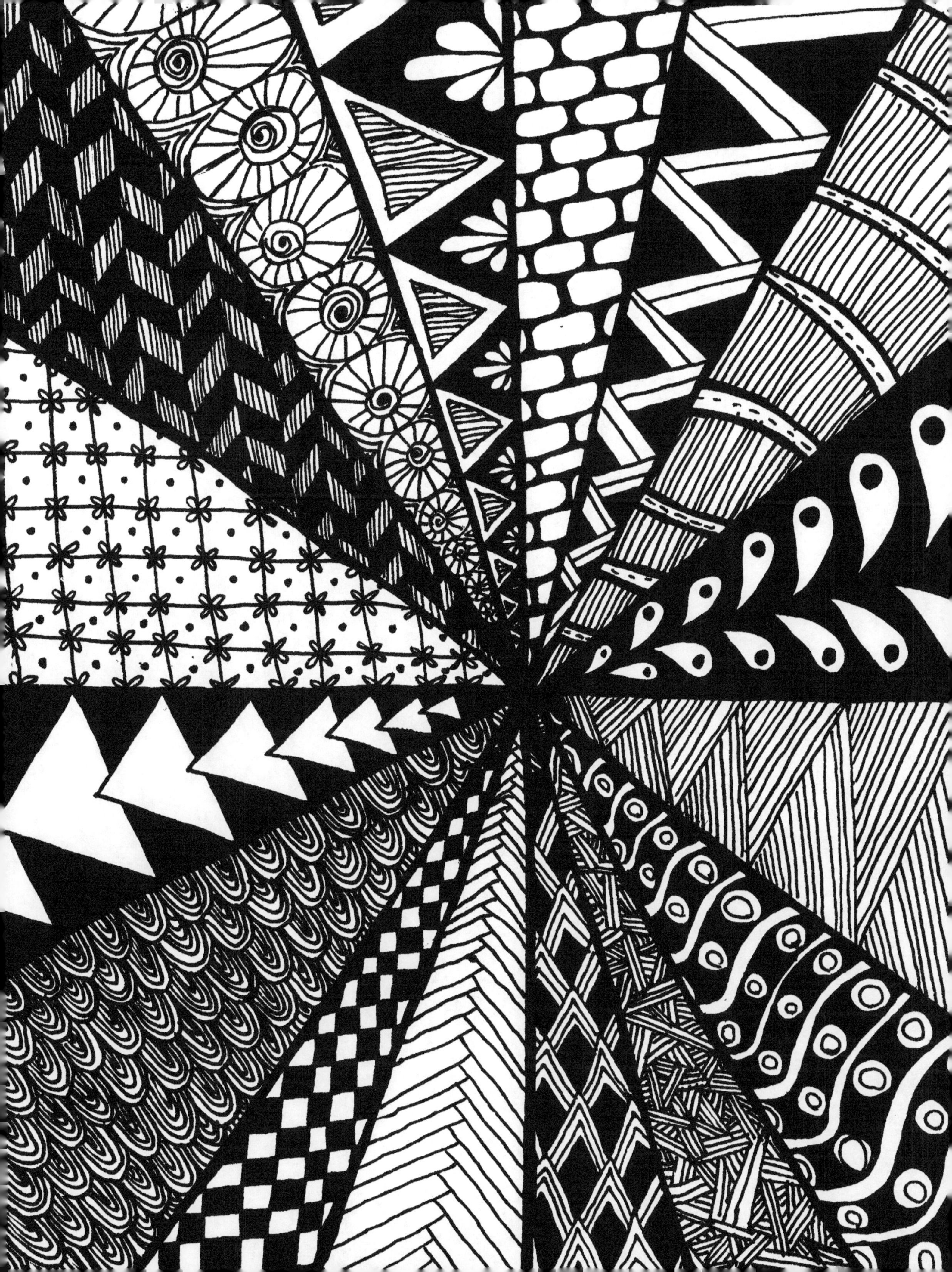

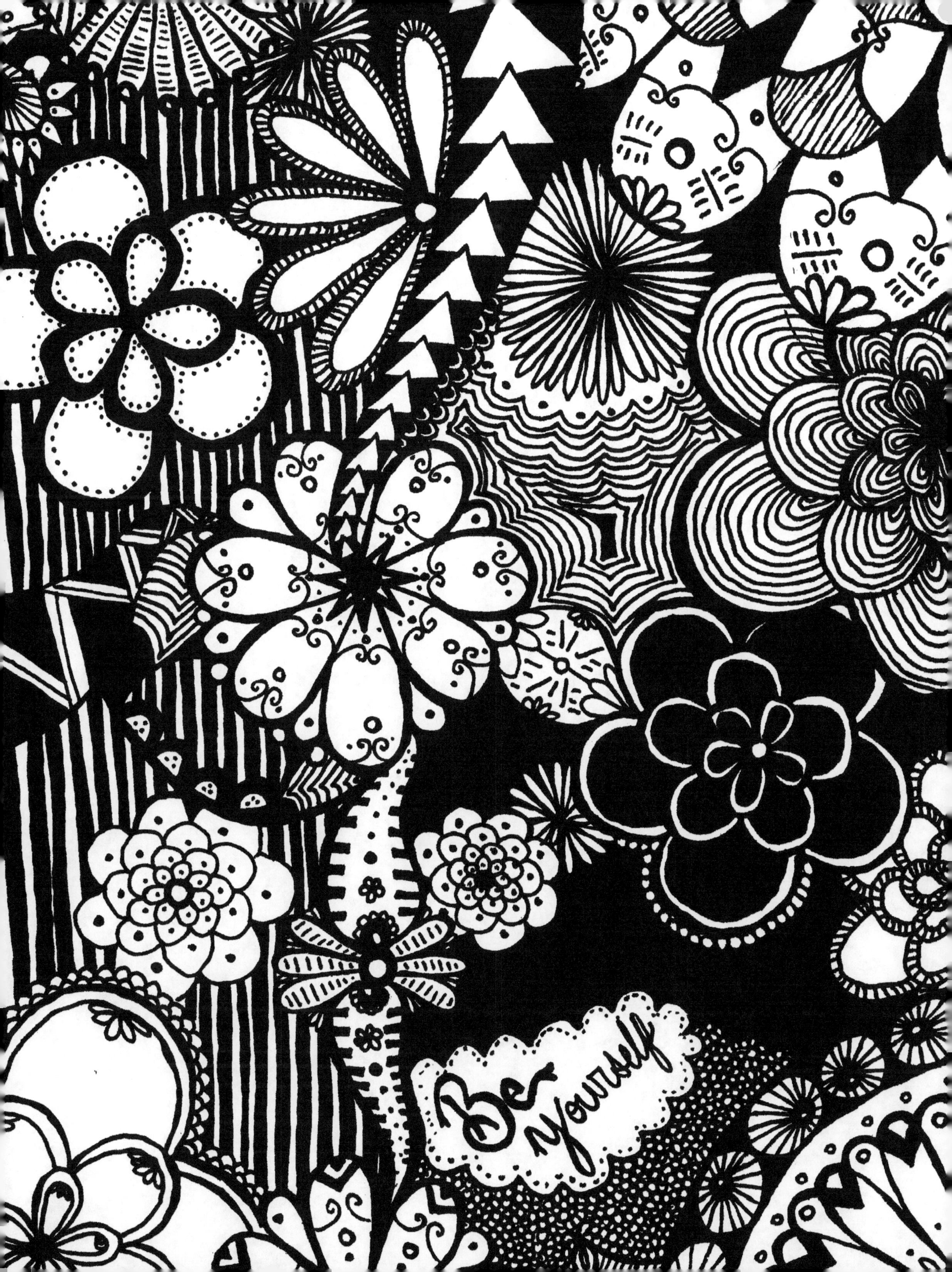
Be yourself

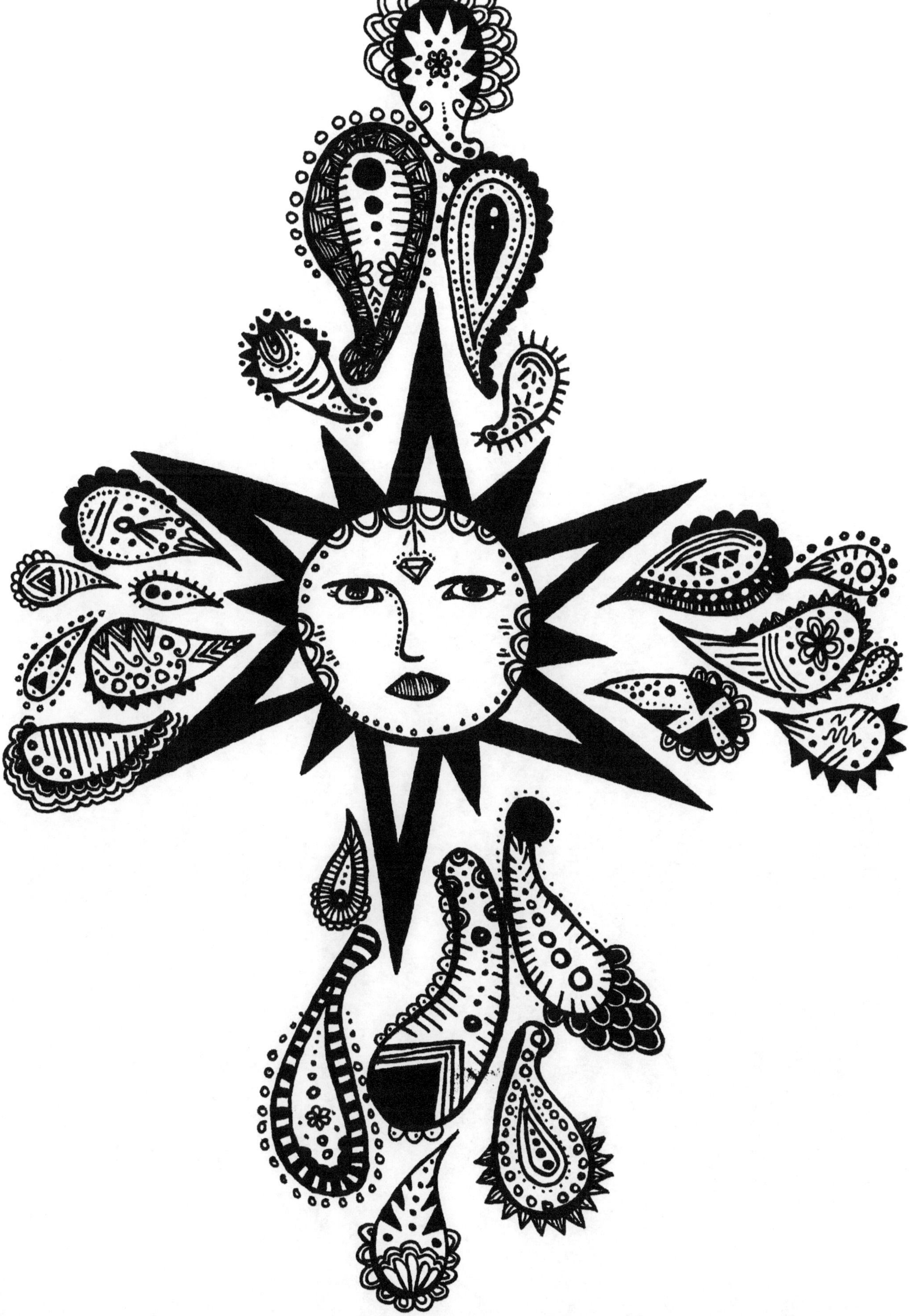

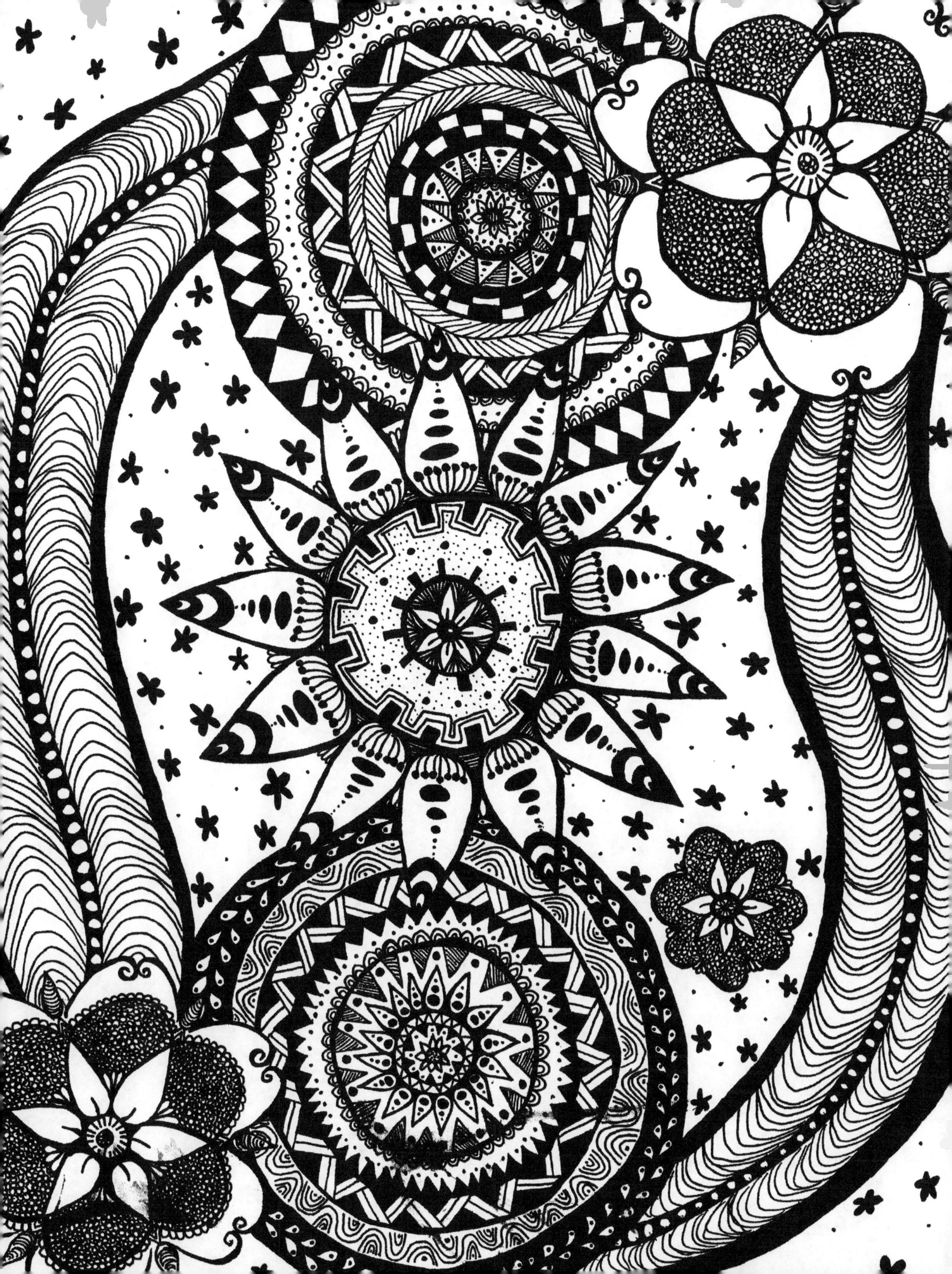

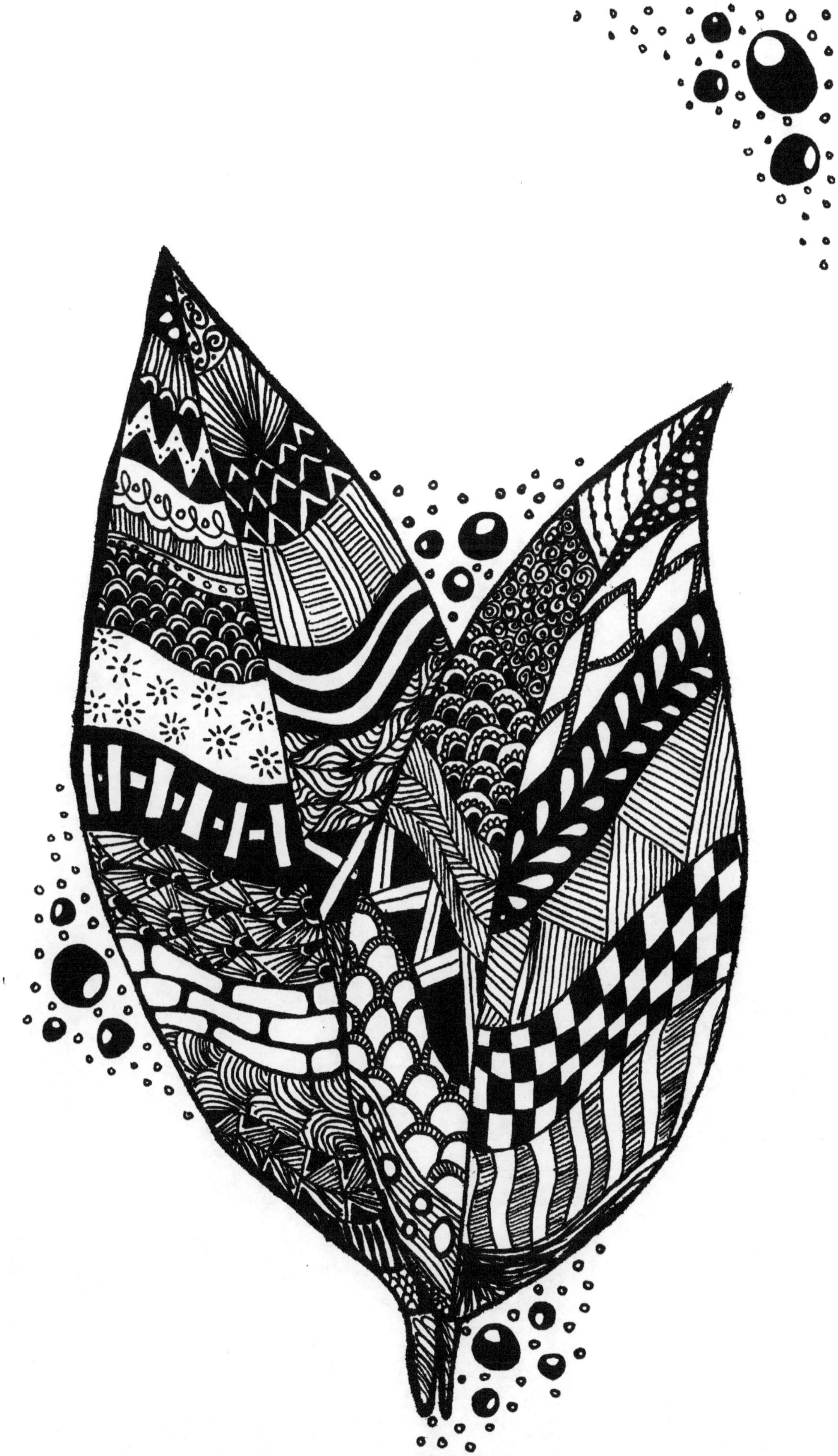

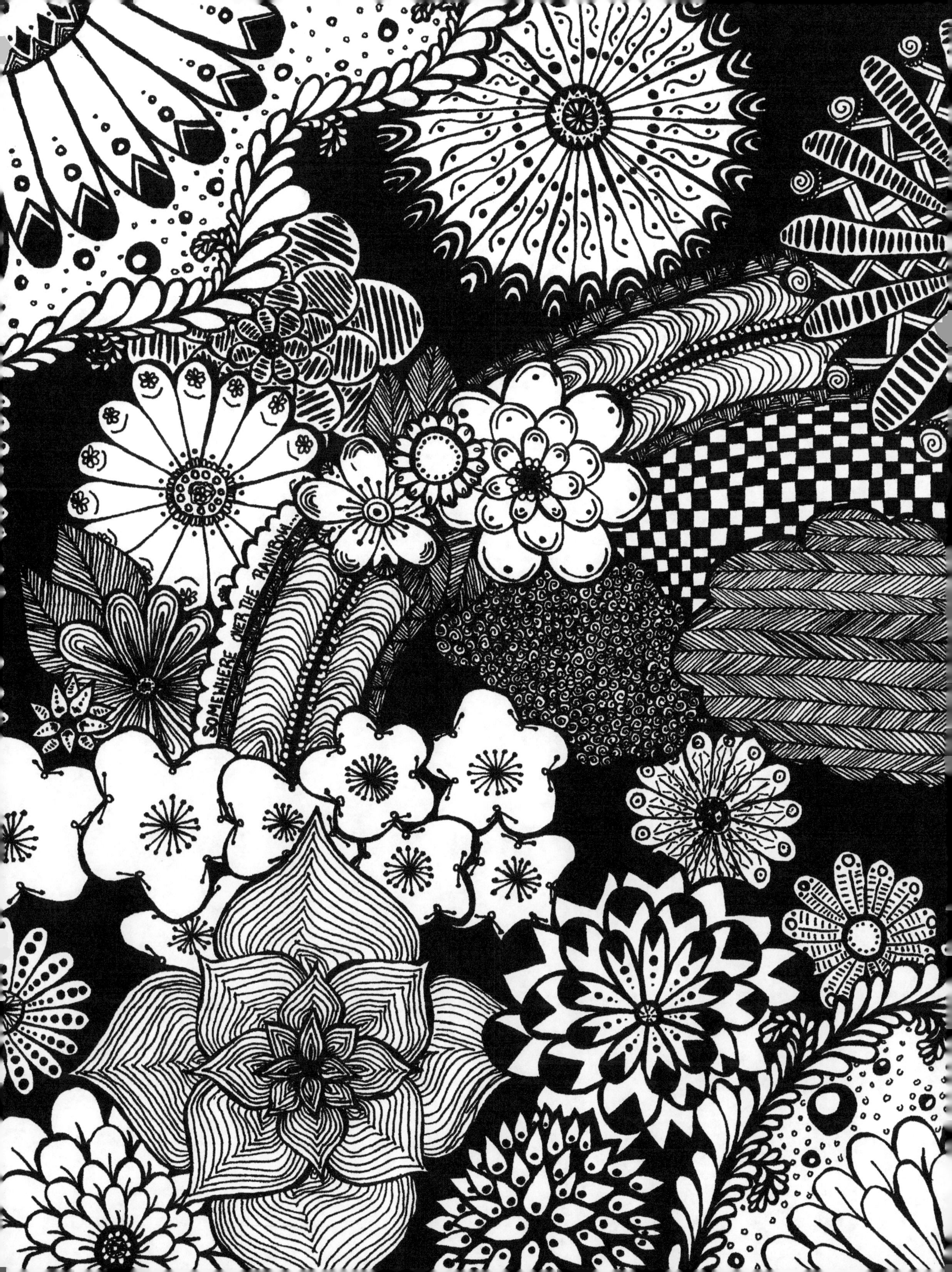
SOMEWHERE OVER THE RAINBOW...

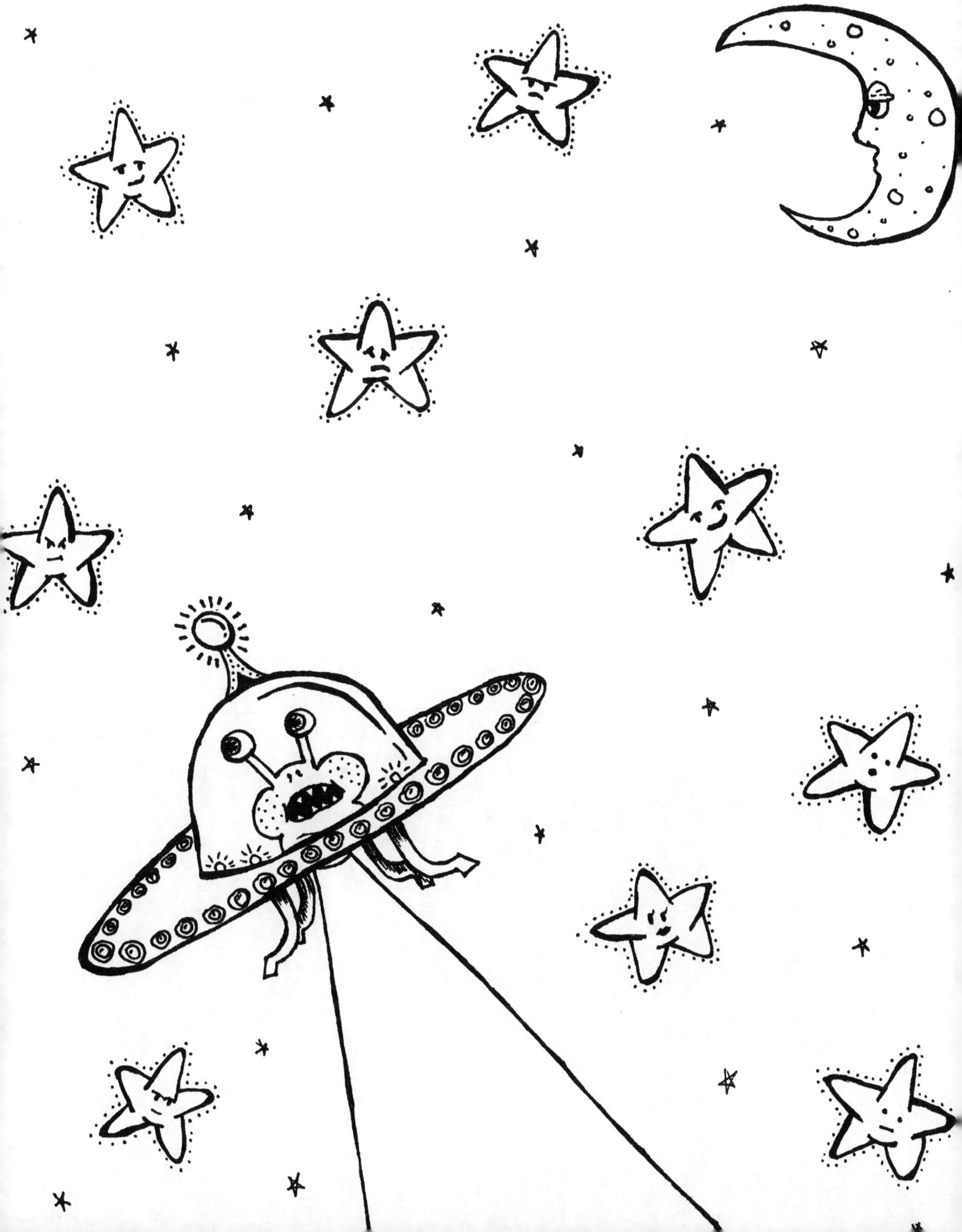

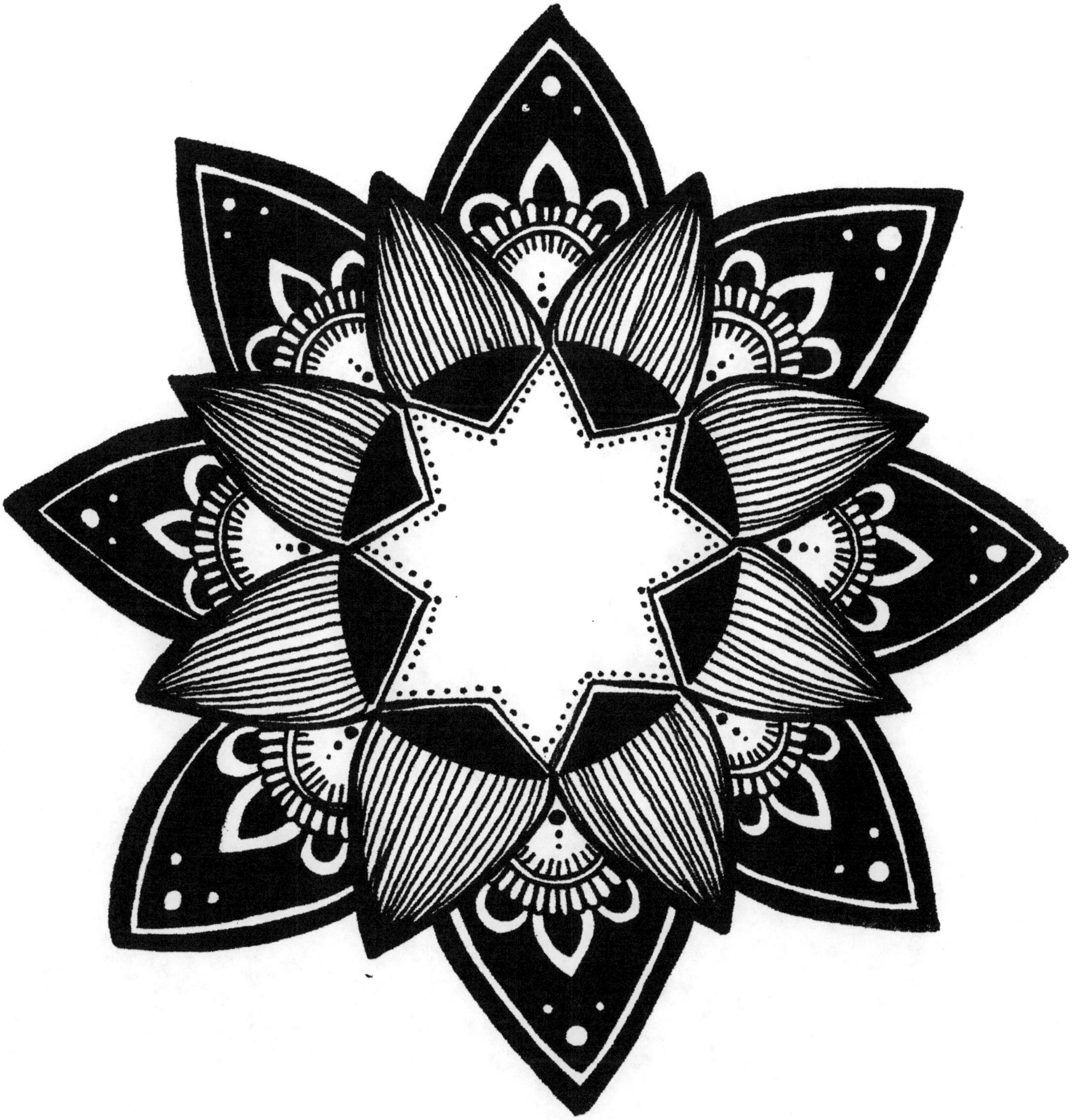

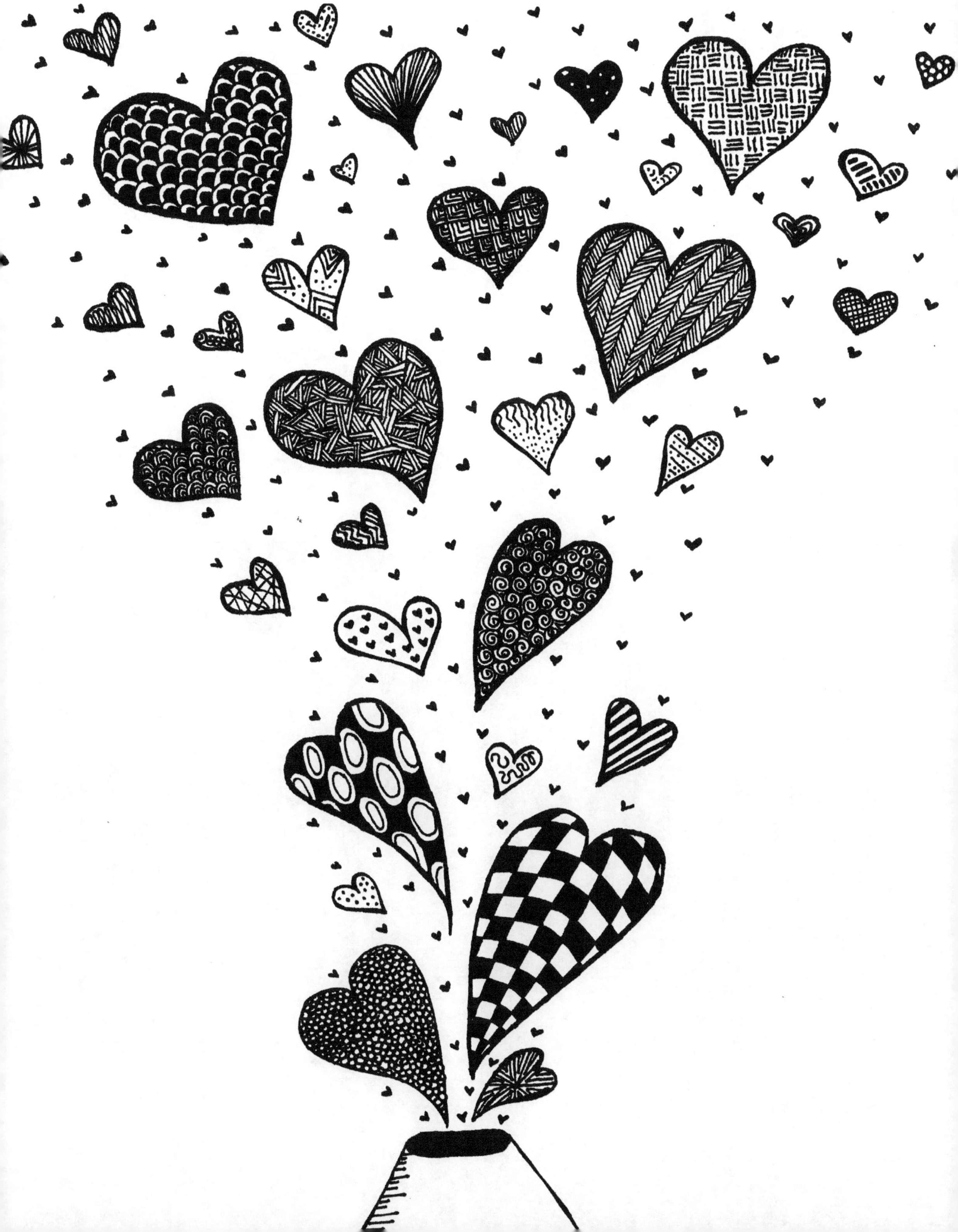

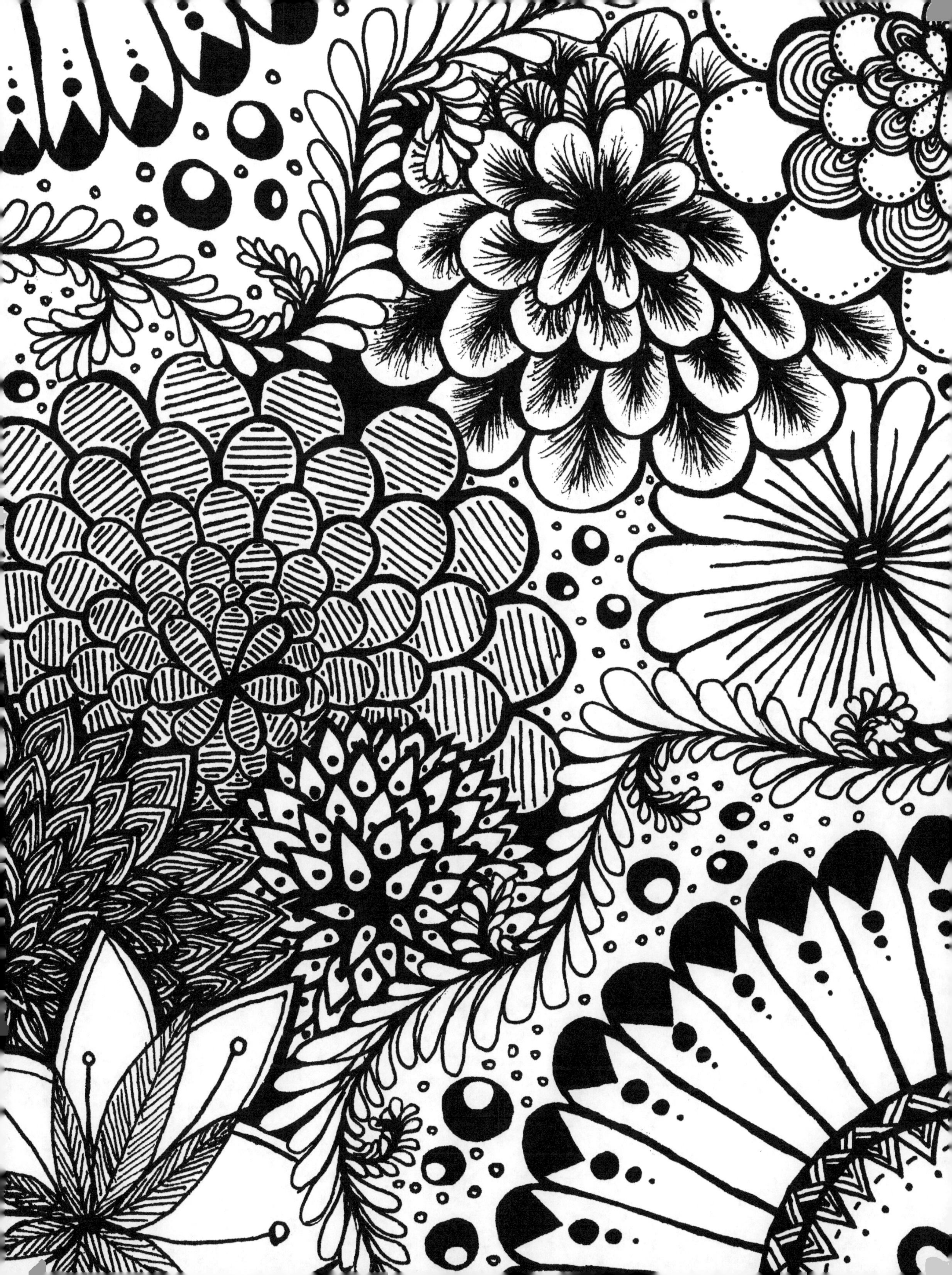

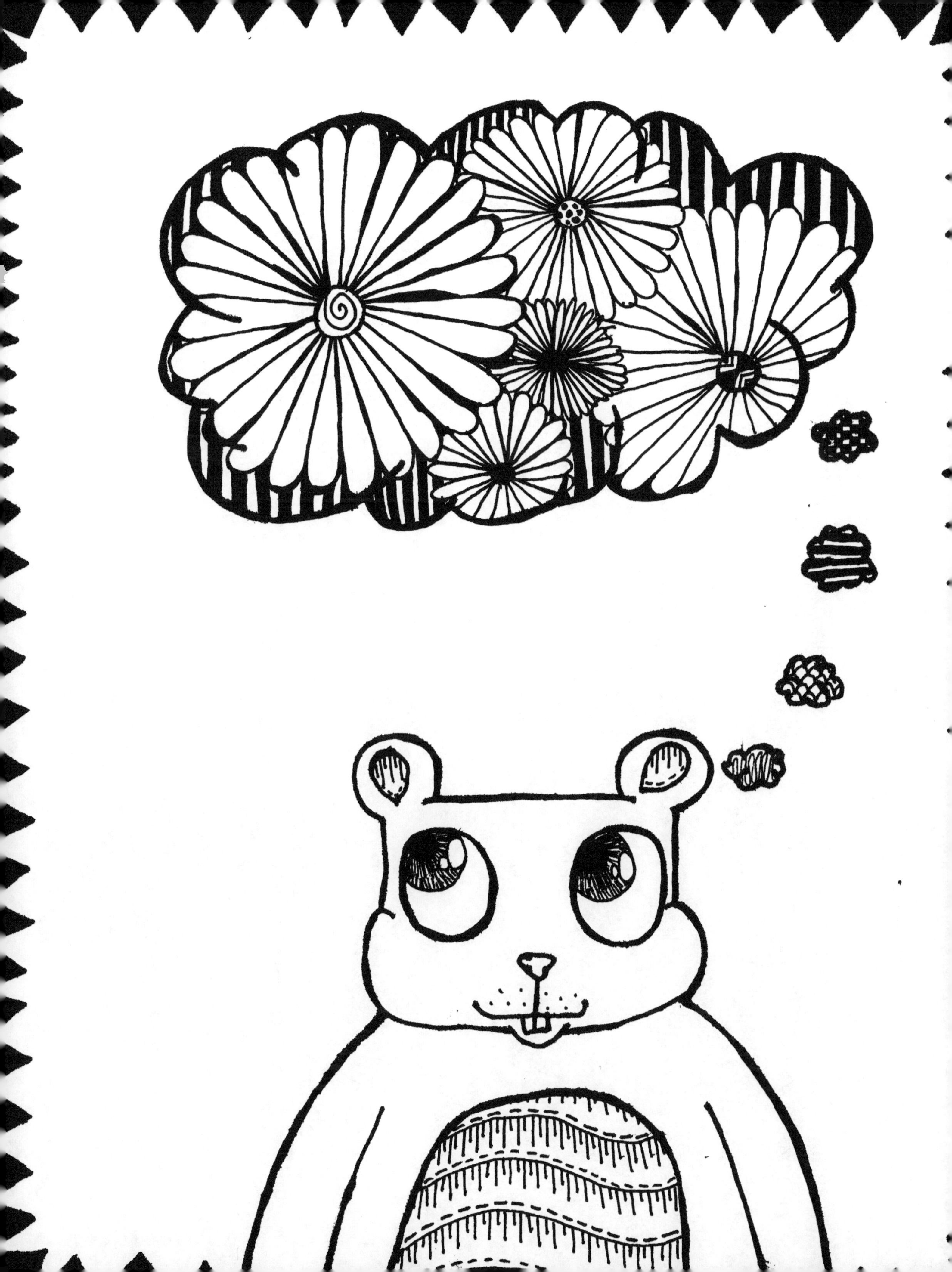

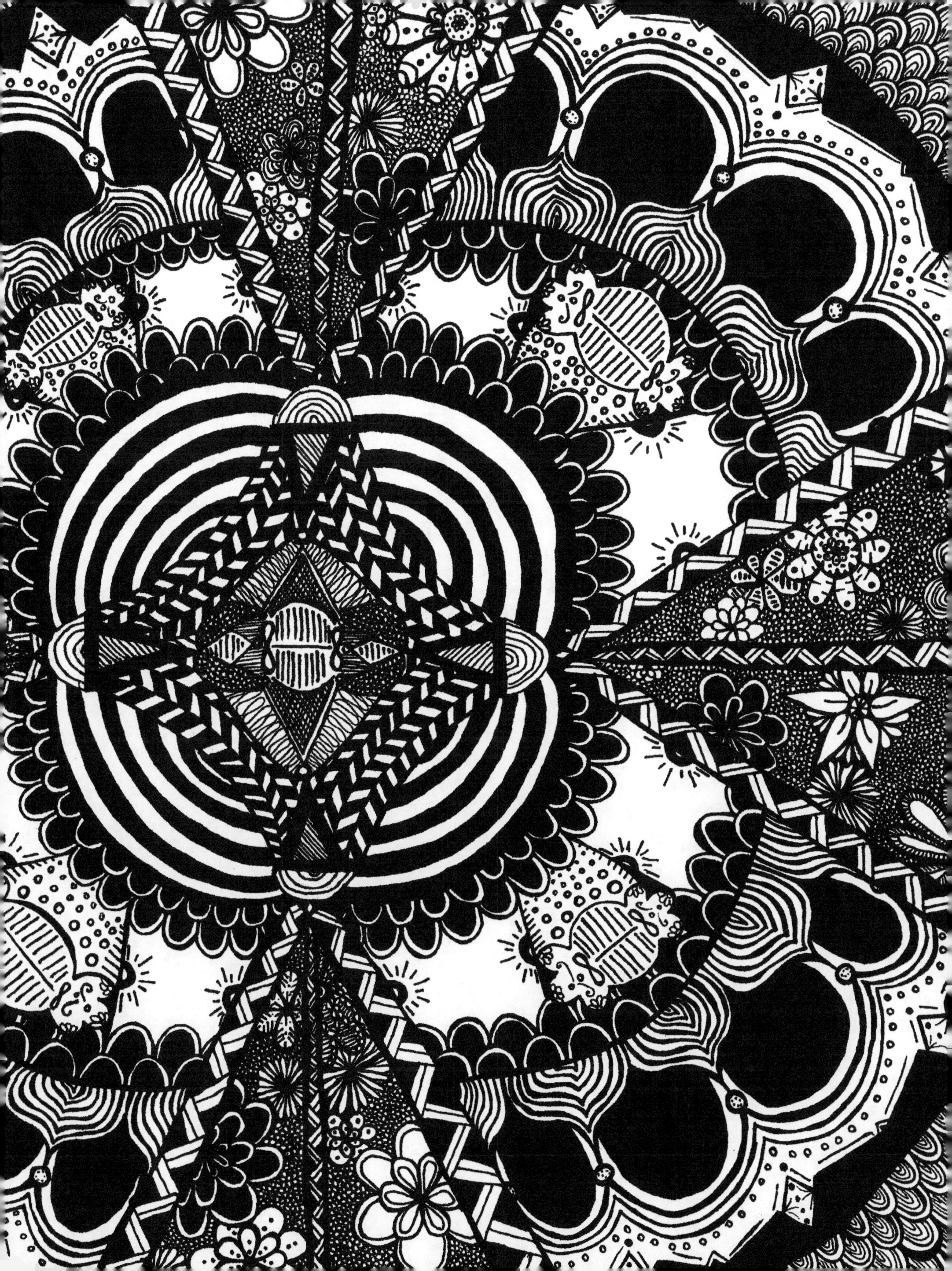

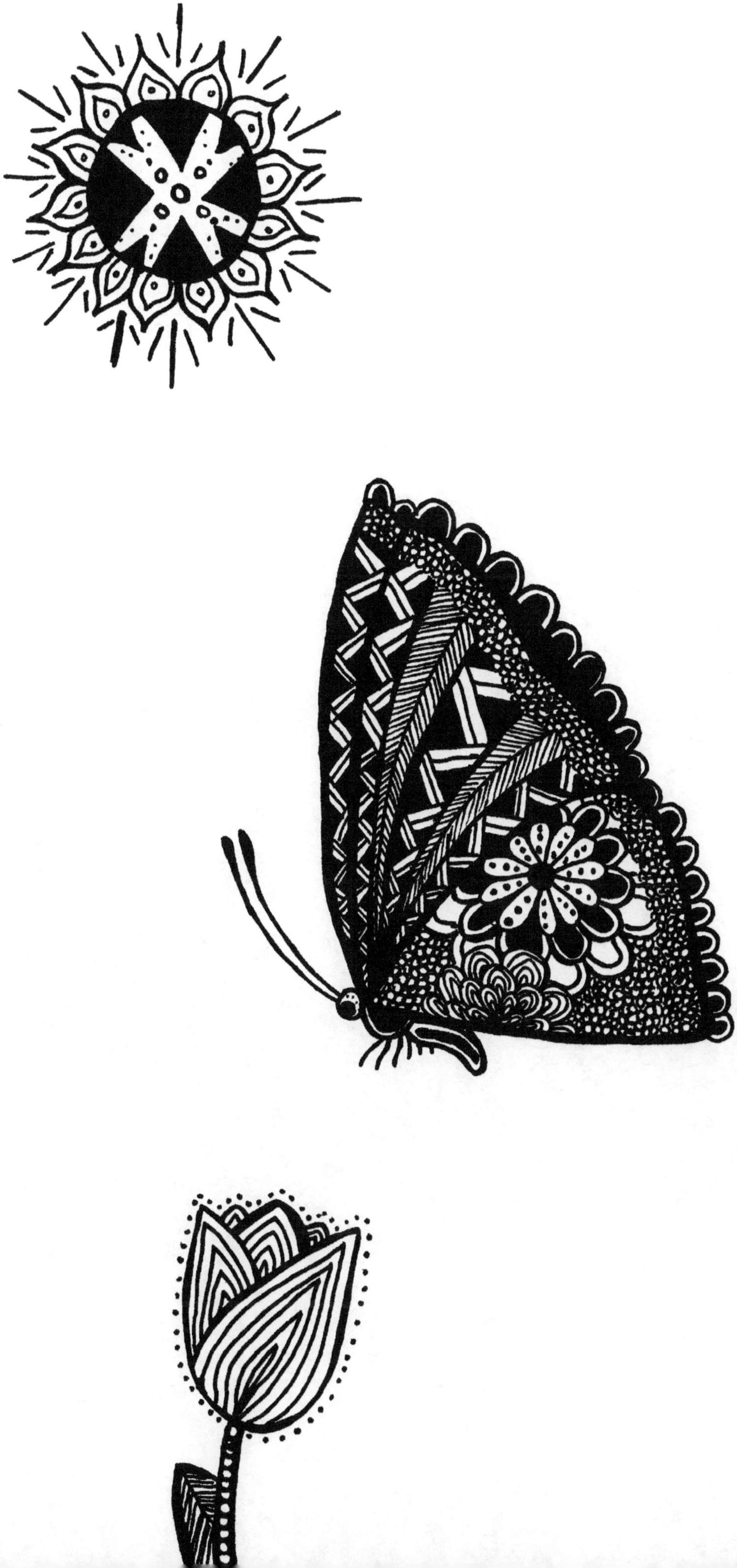

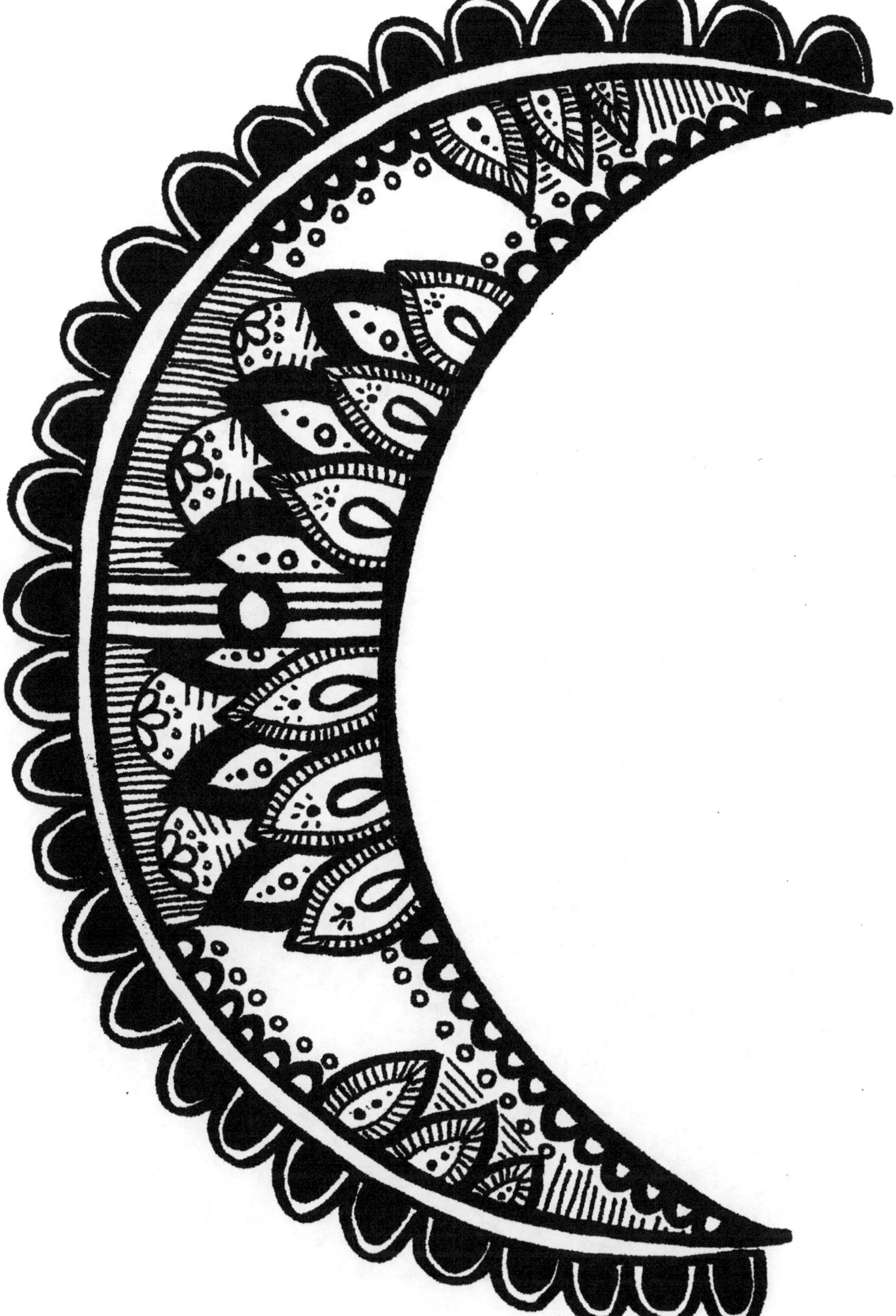

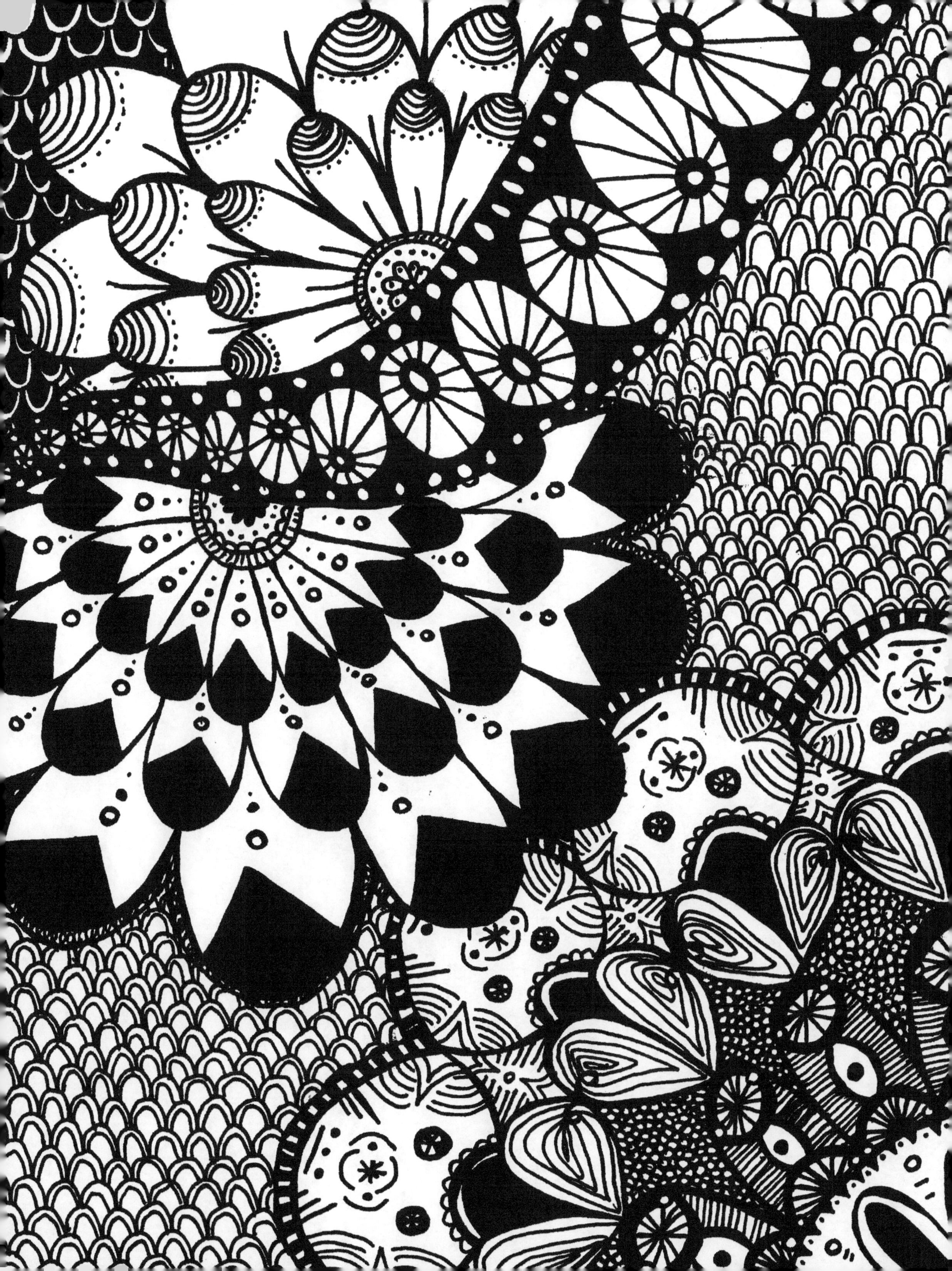

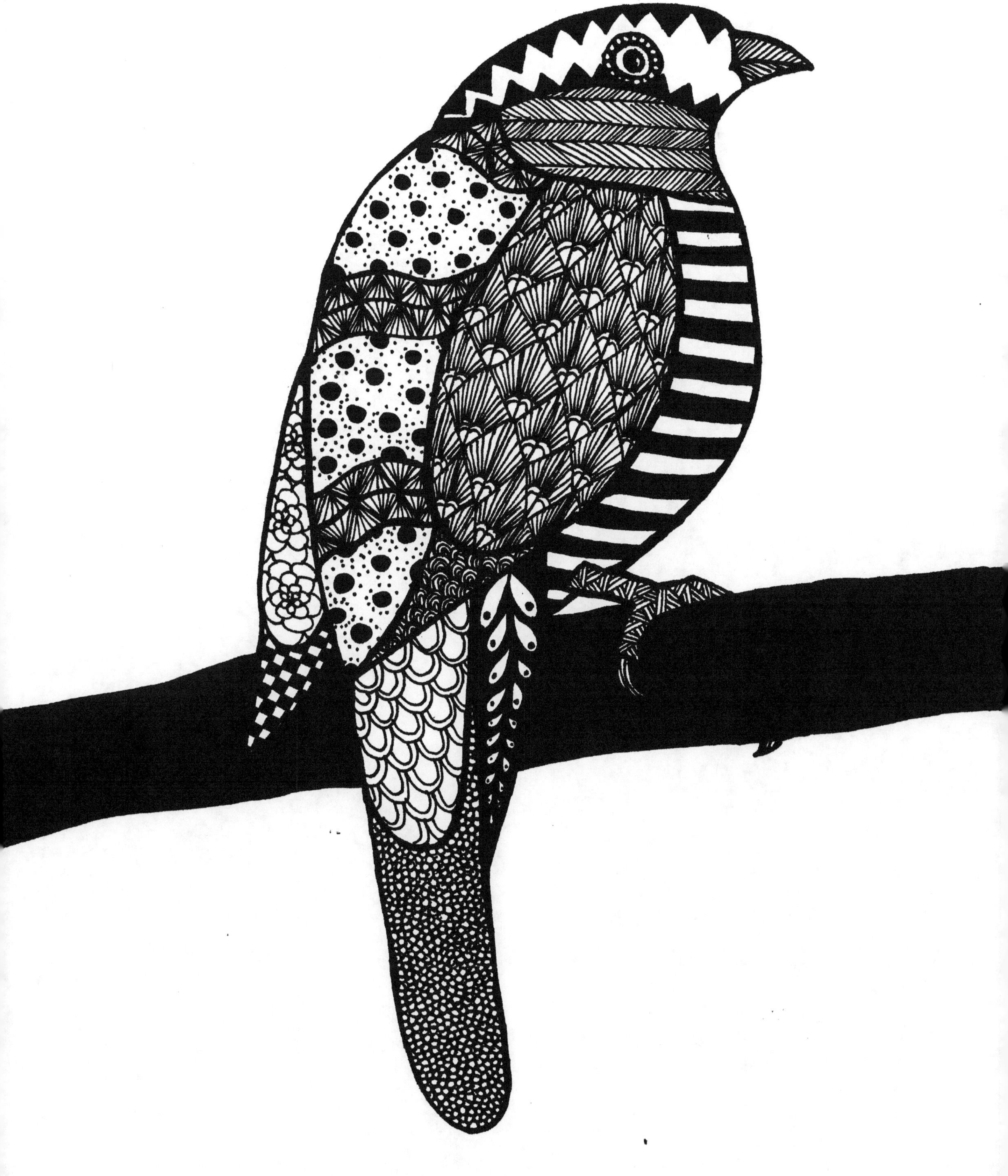

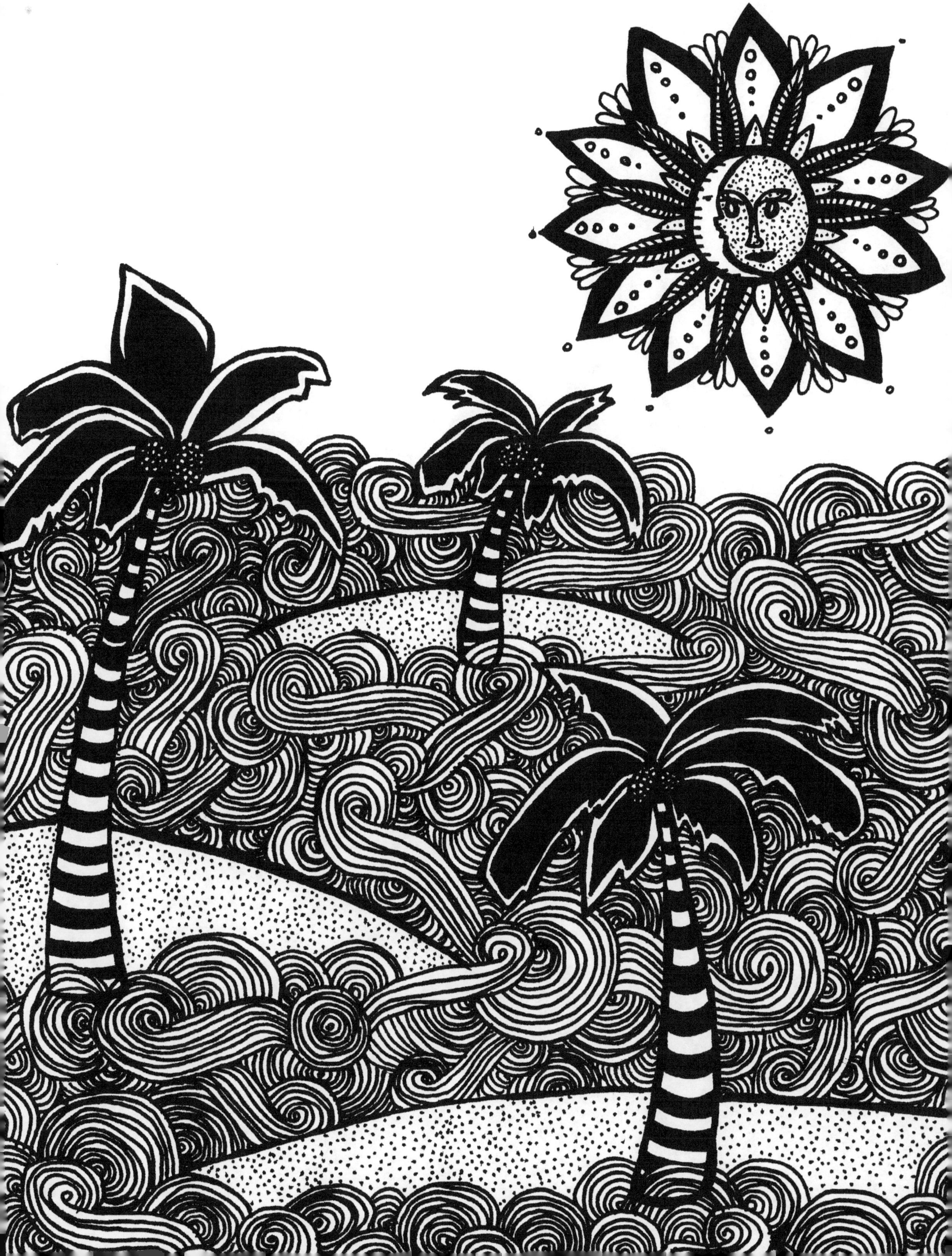

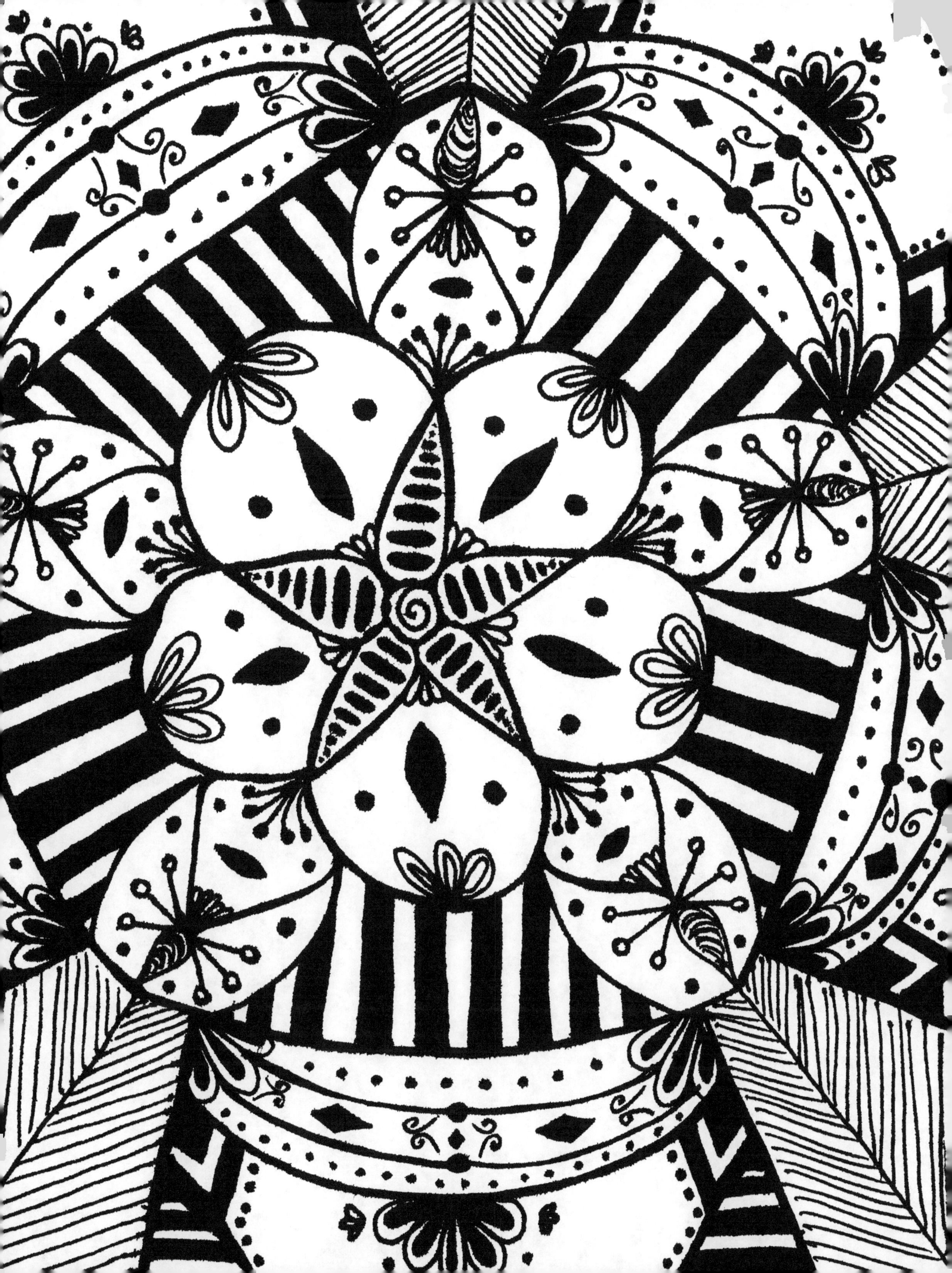

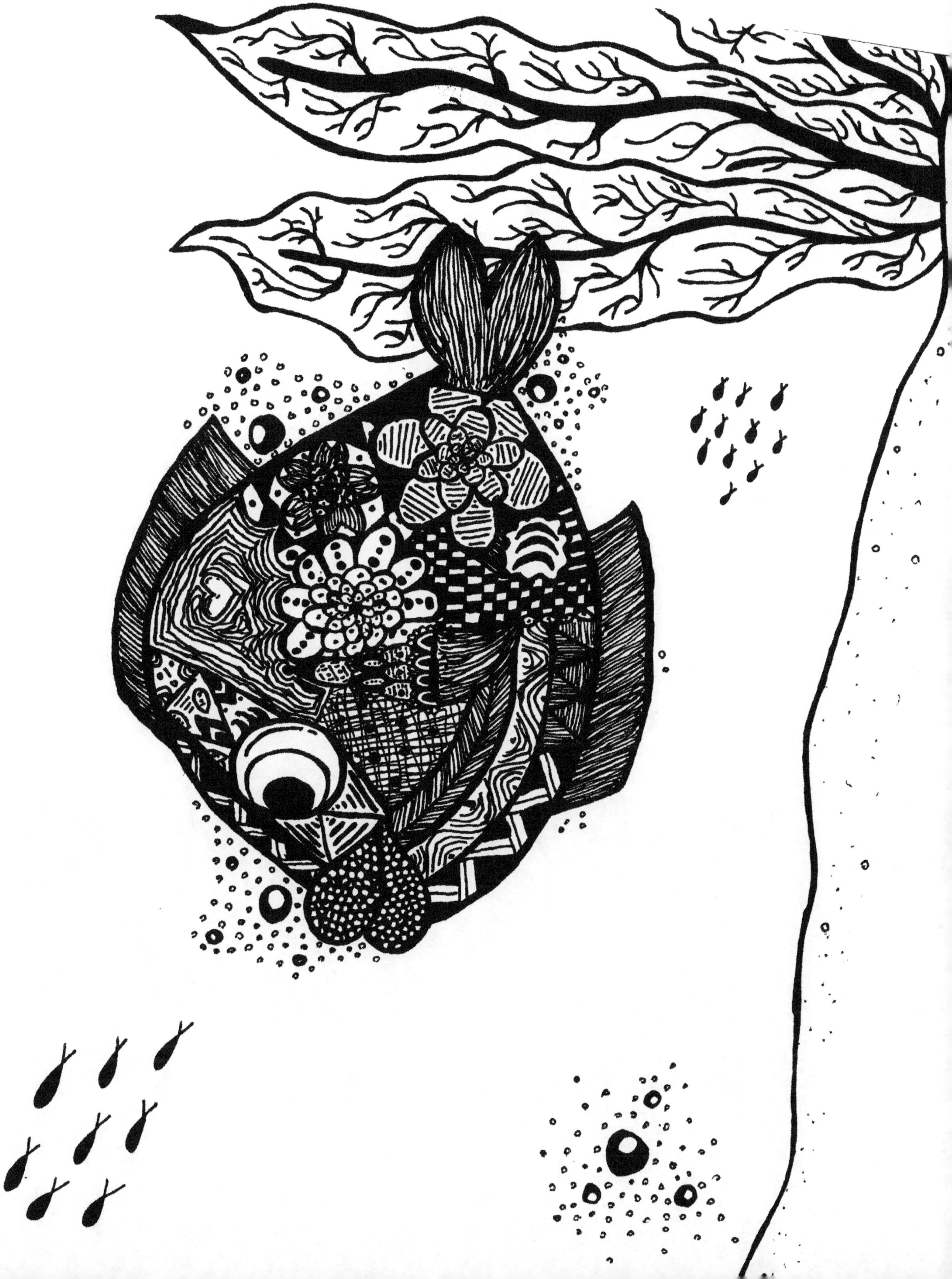

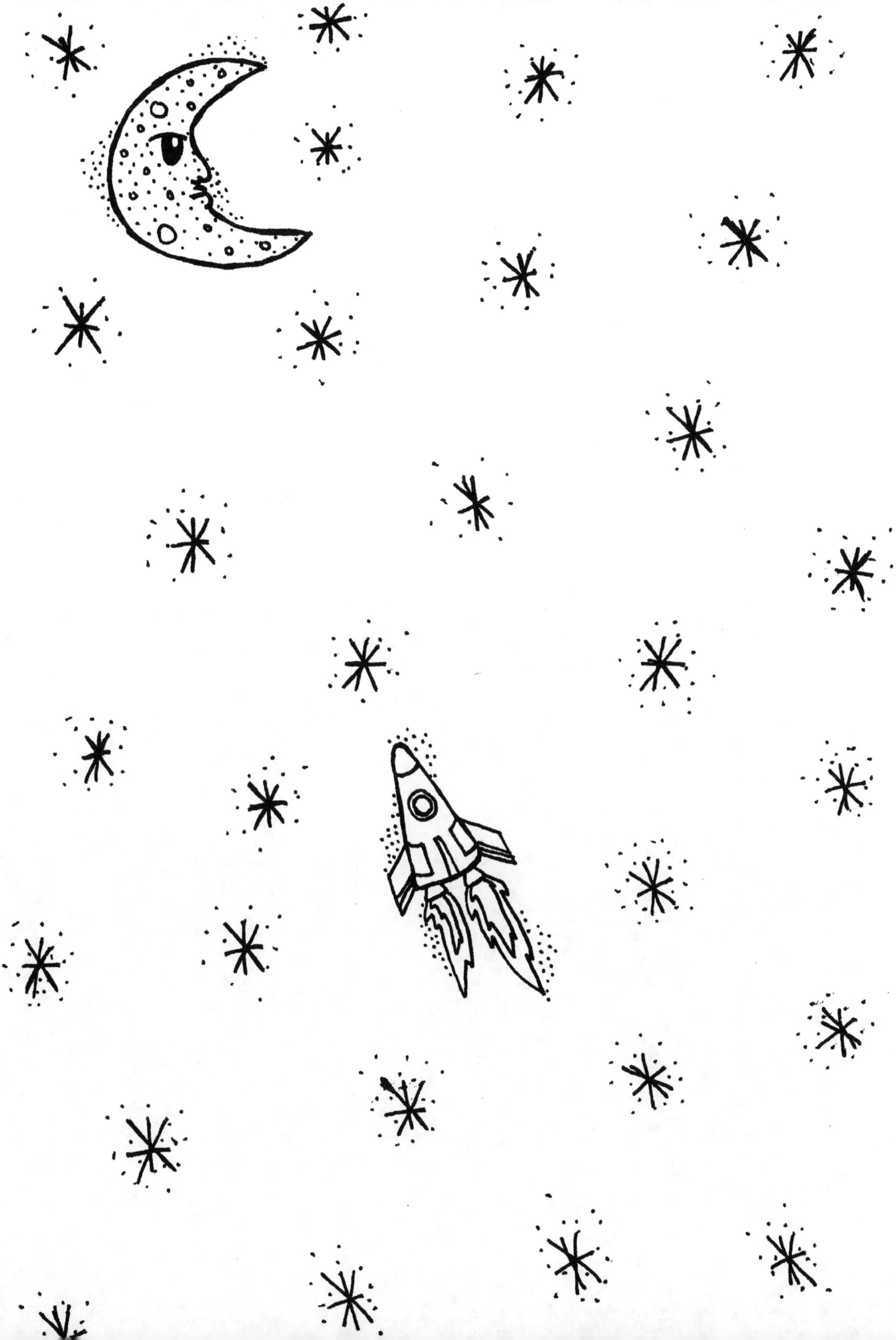

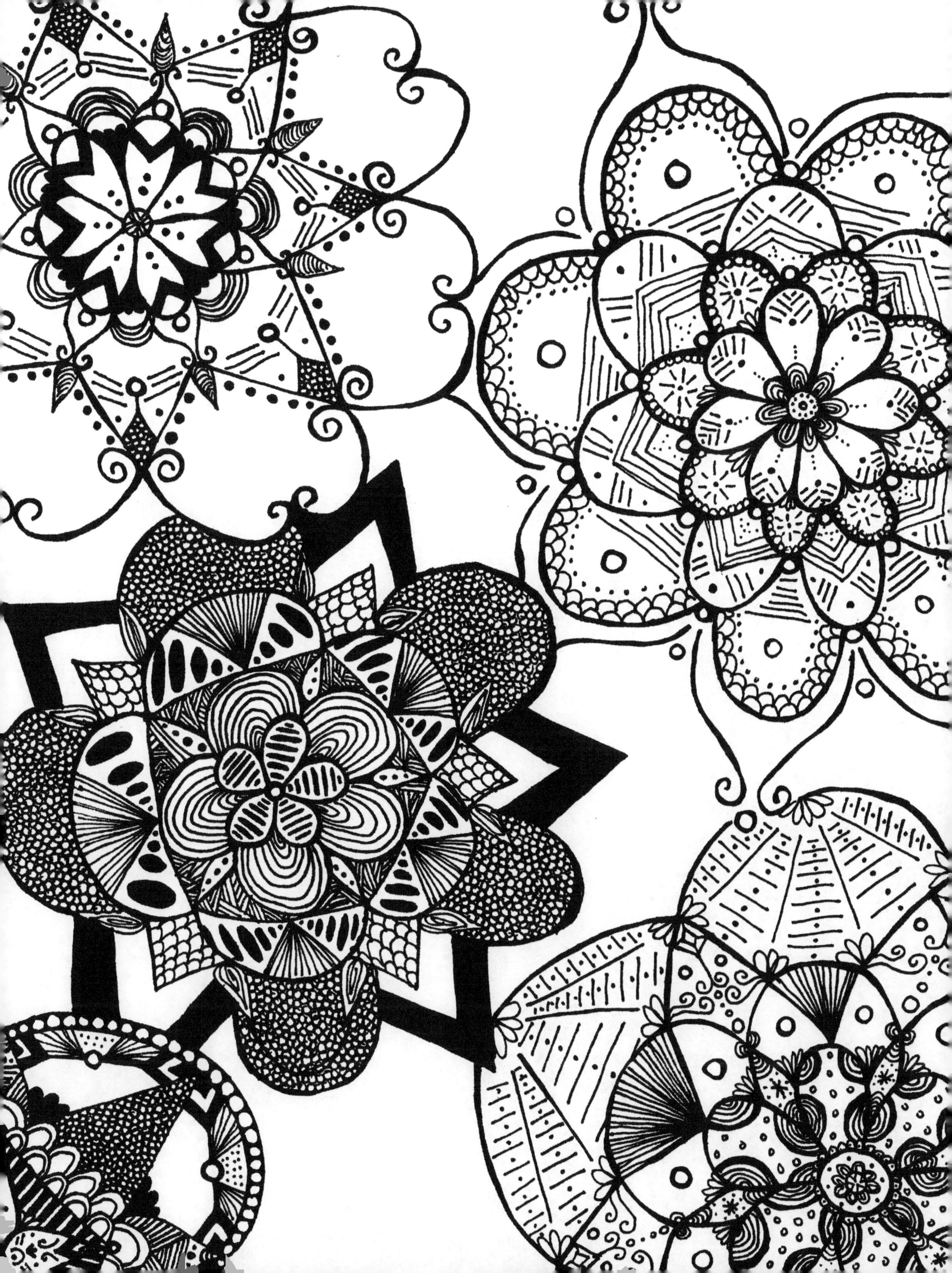

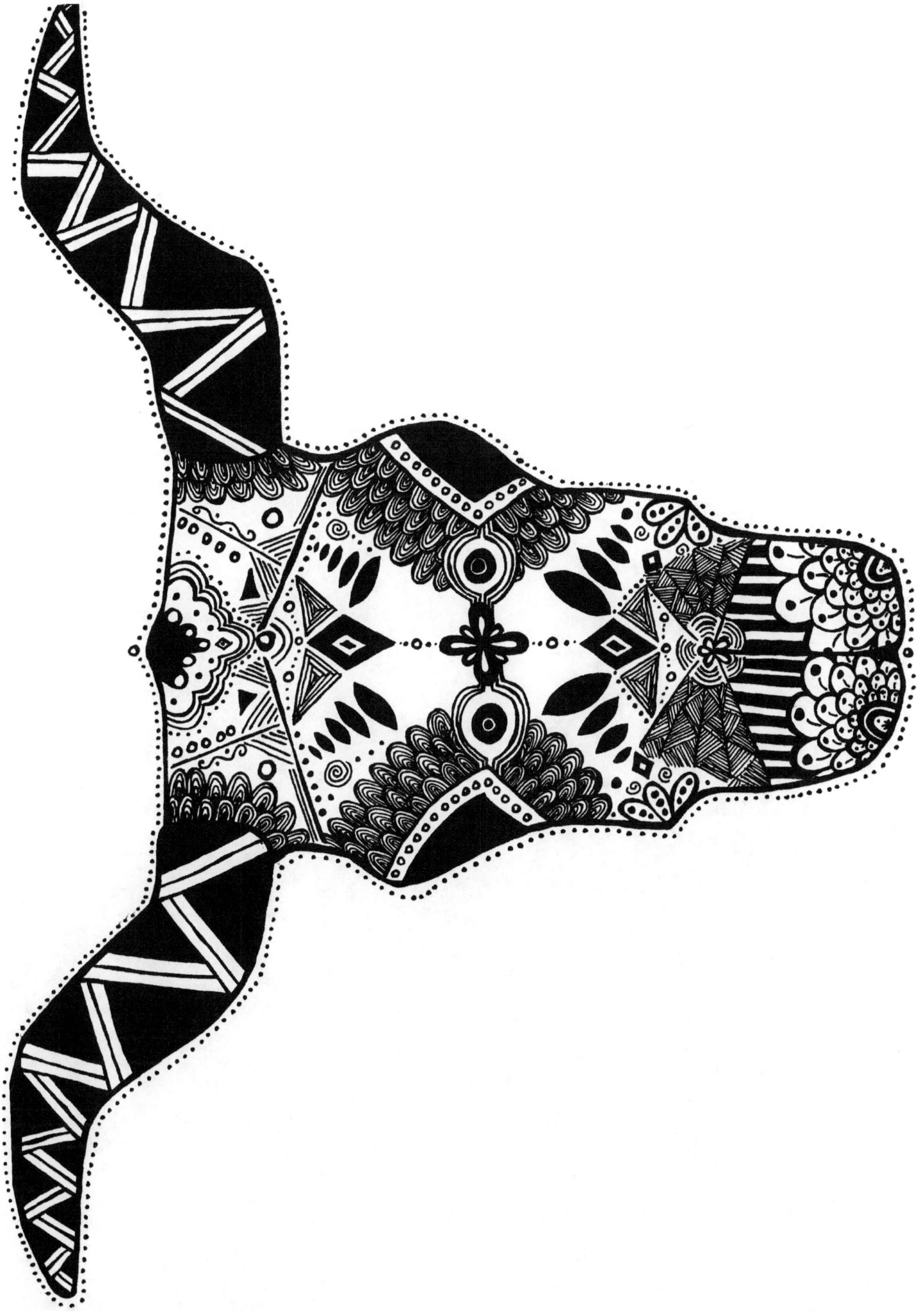

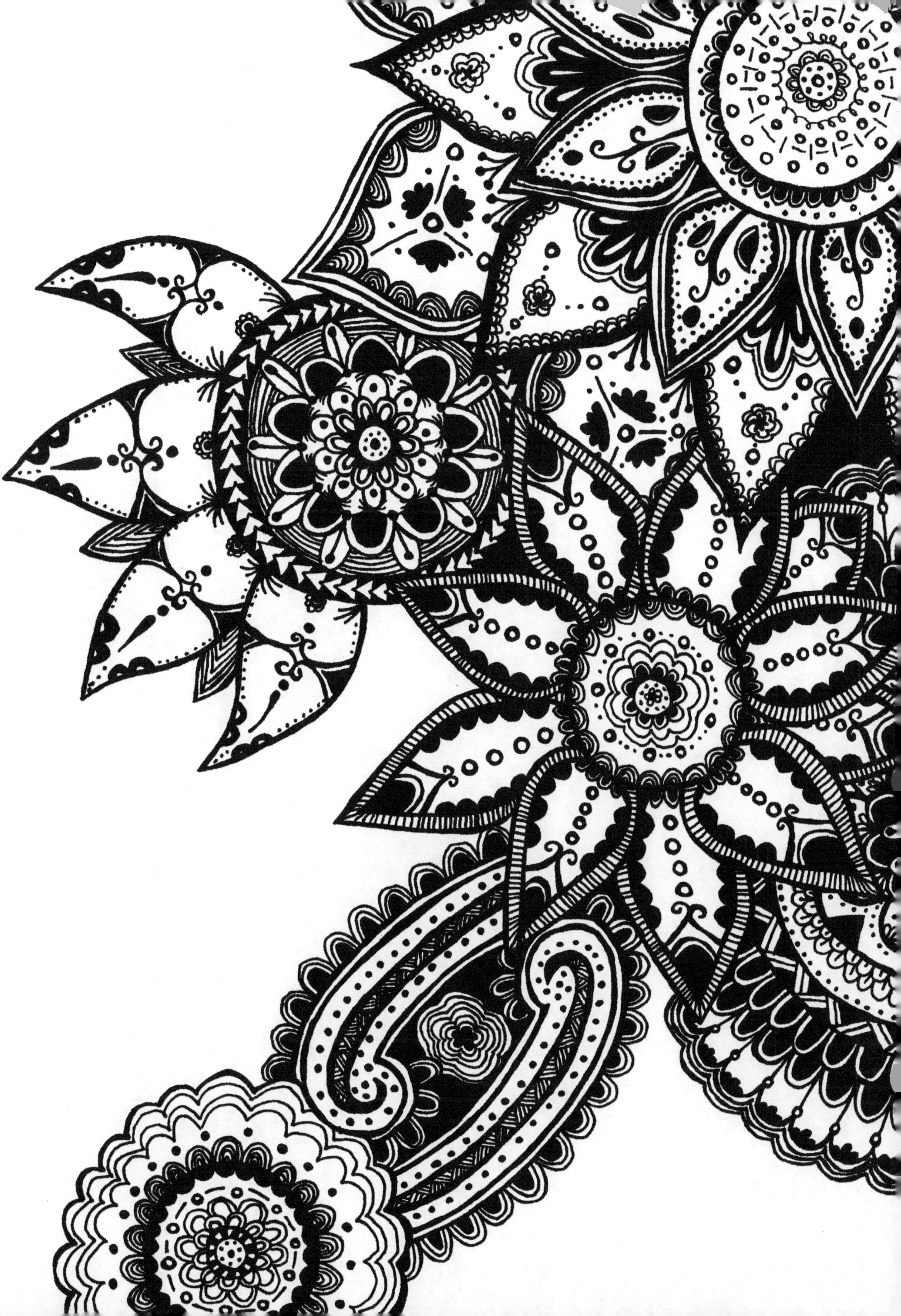

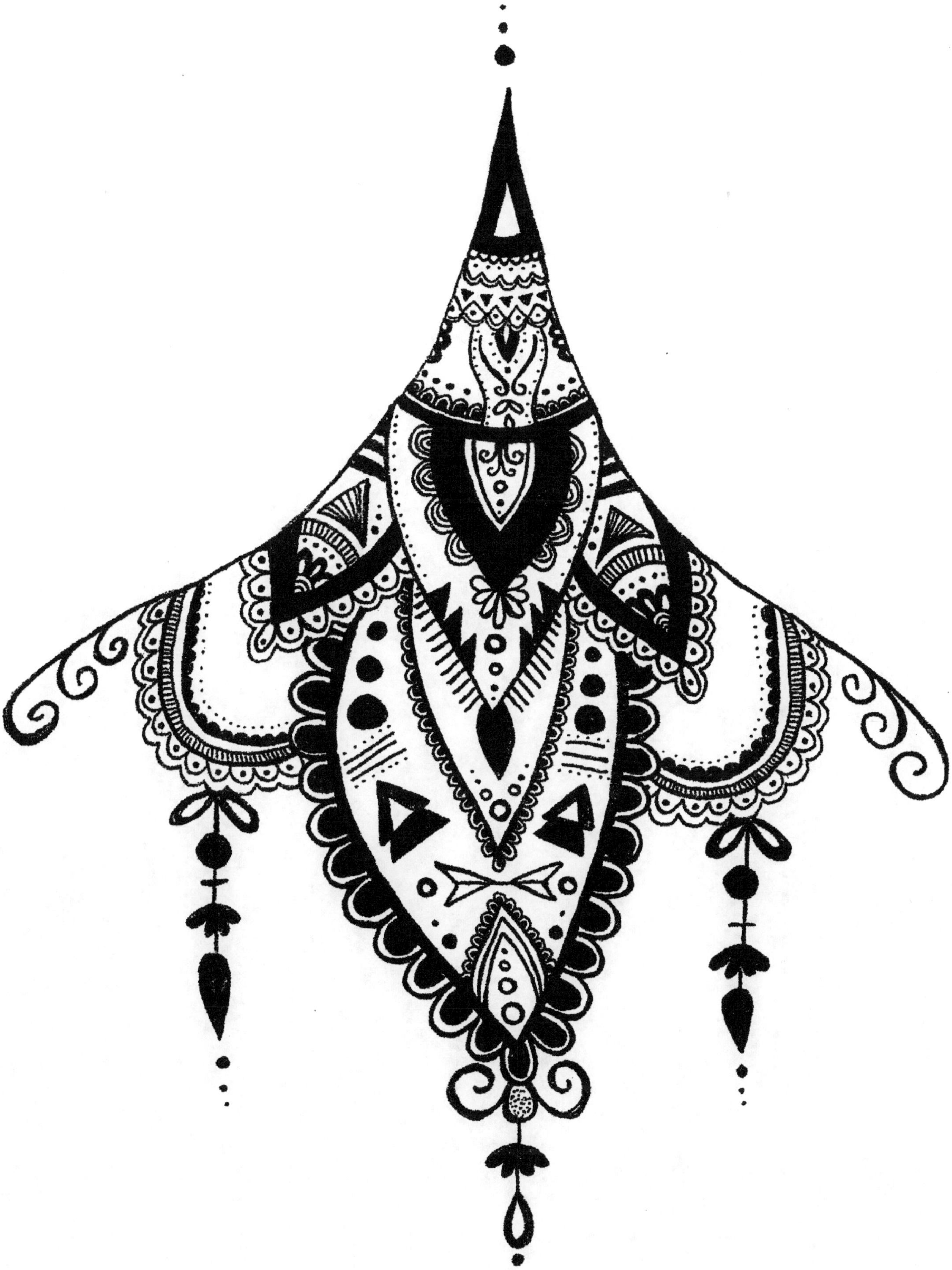

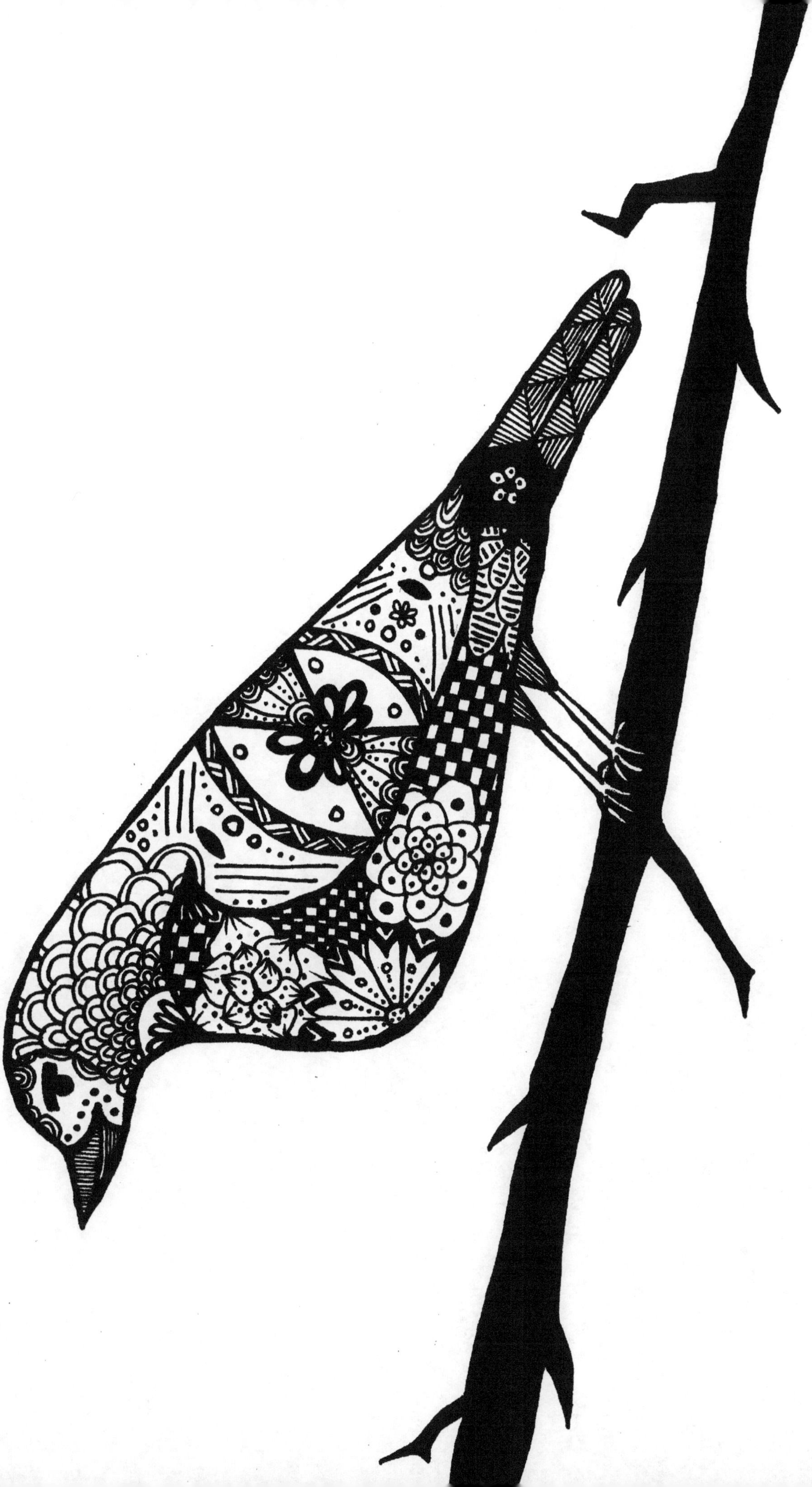

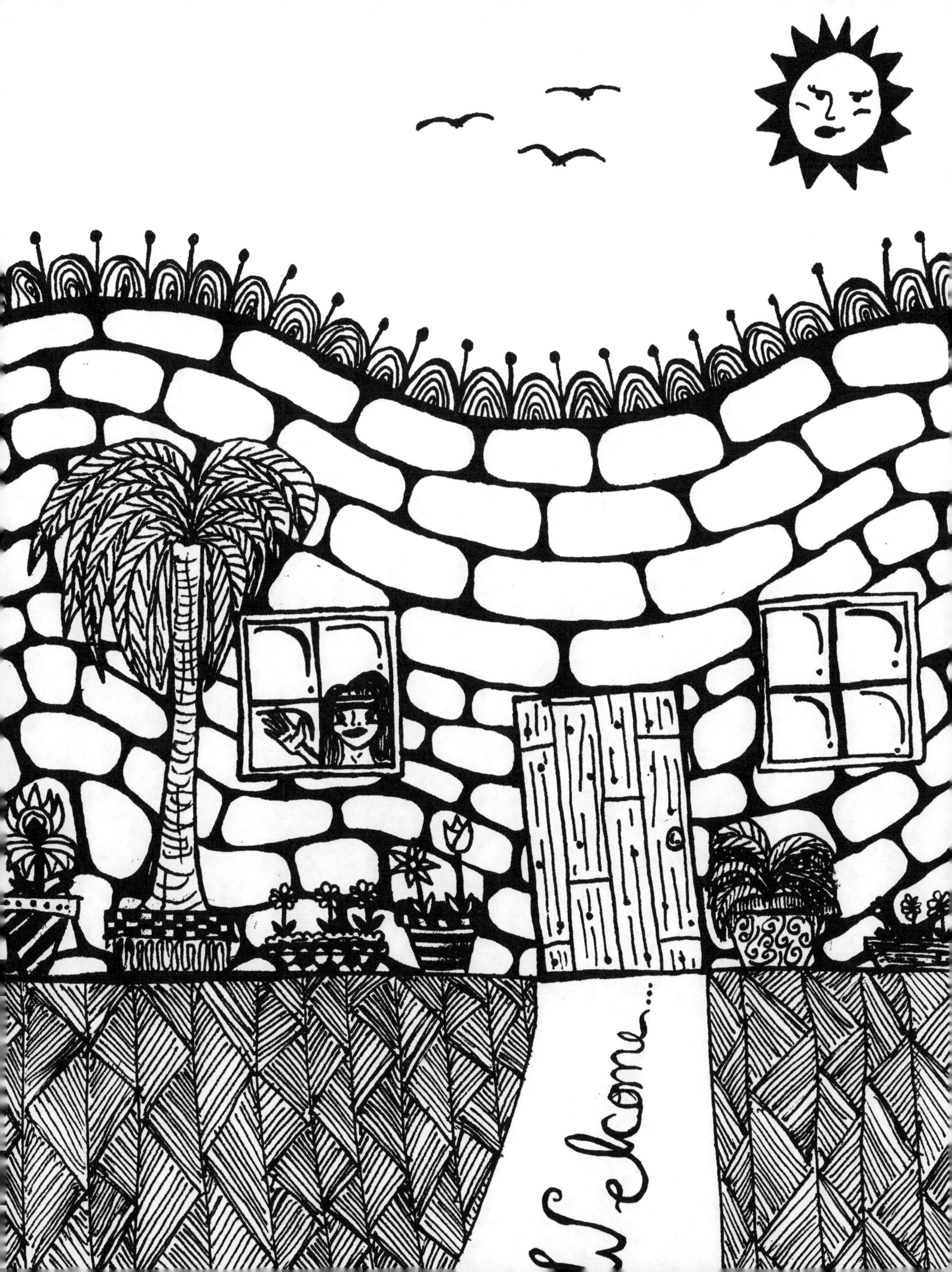
Welcome...

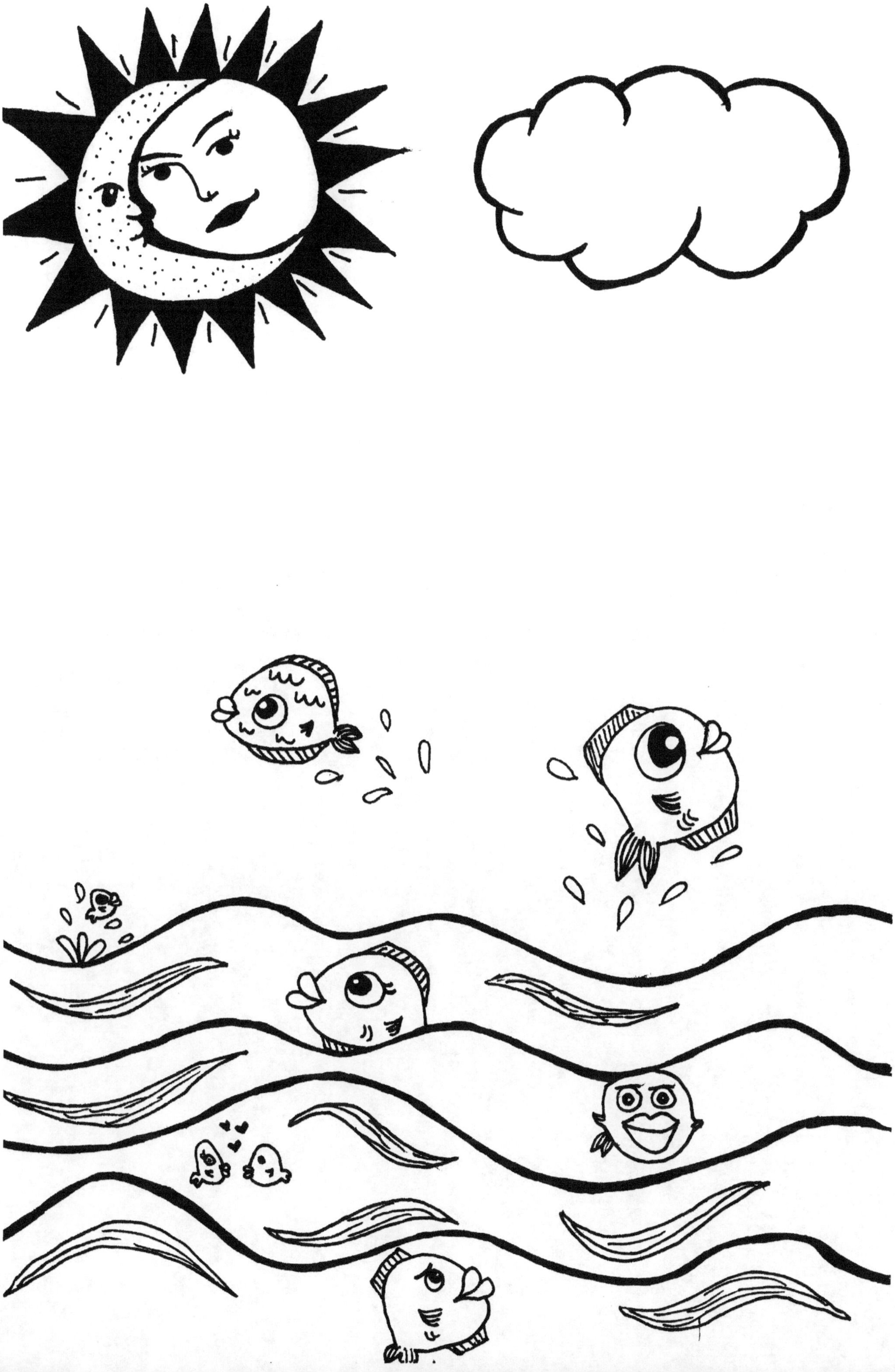

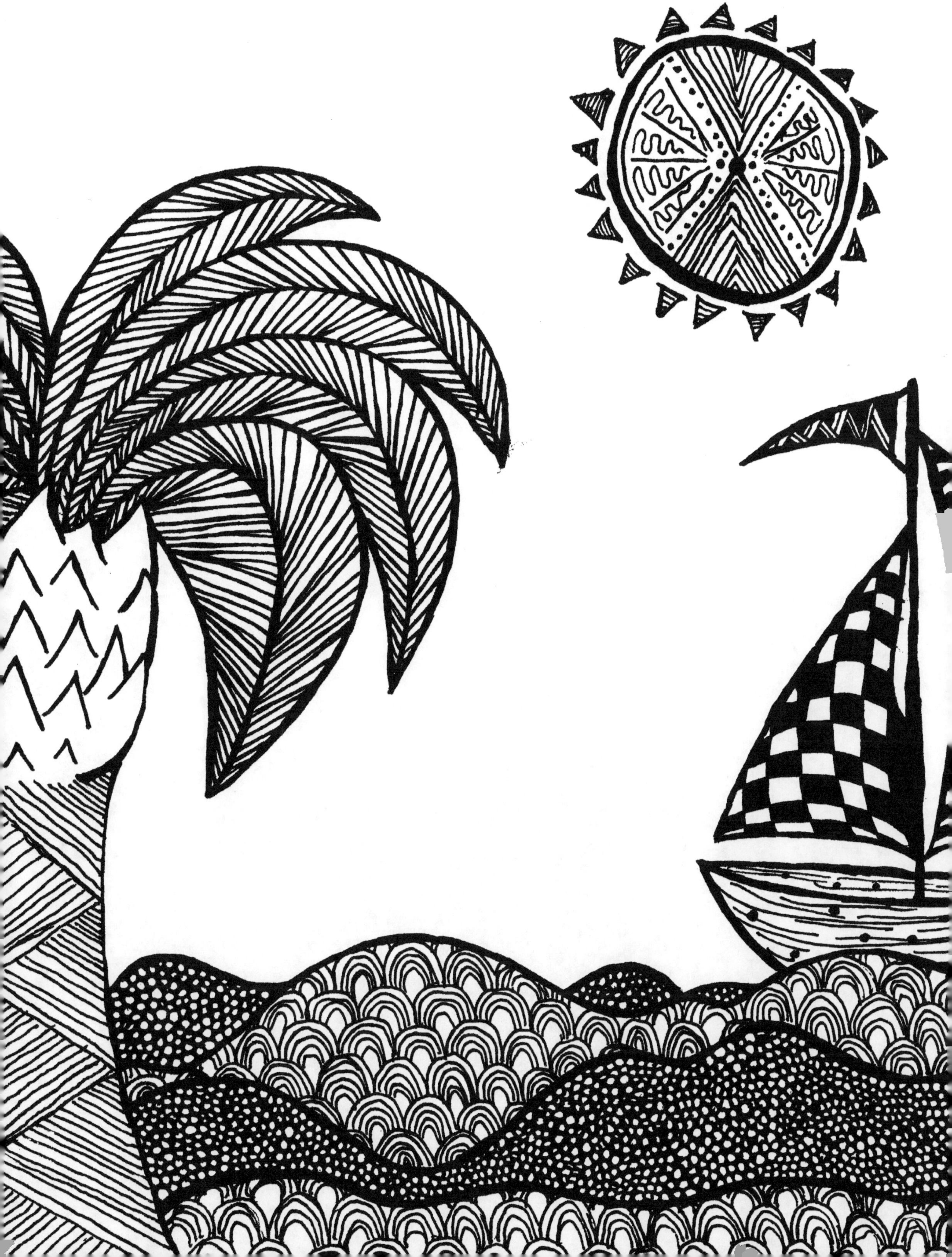

SOME

see a

WEED

SOME

see a

WISH.

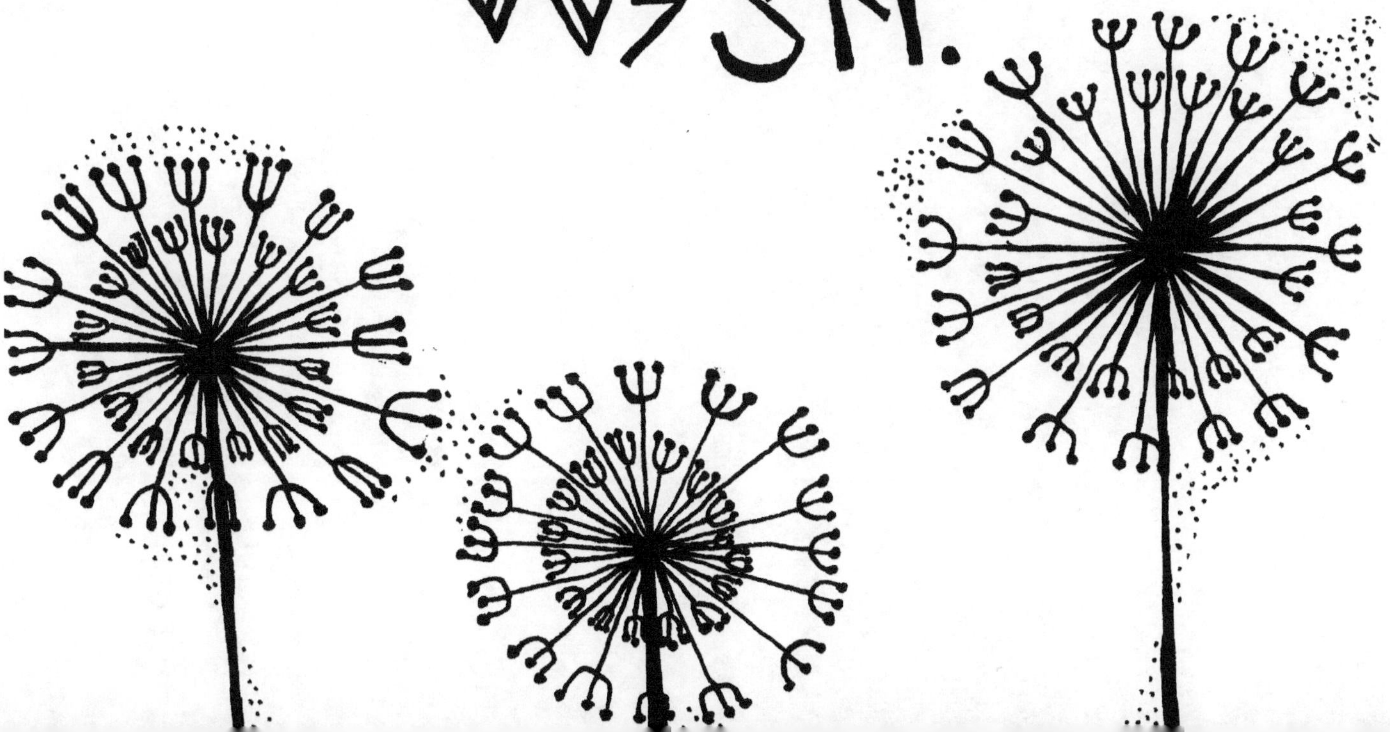

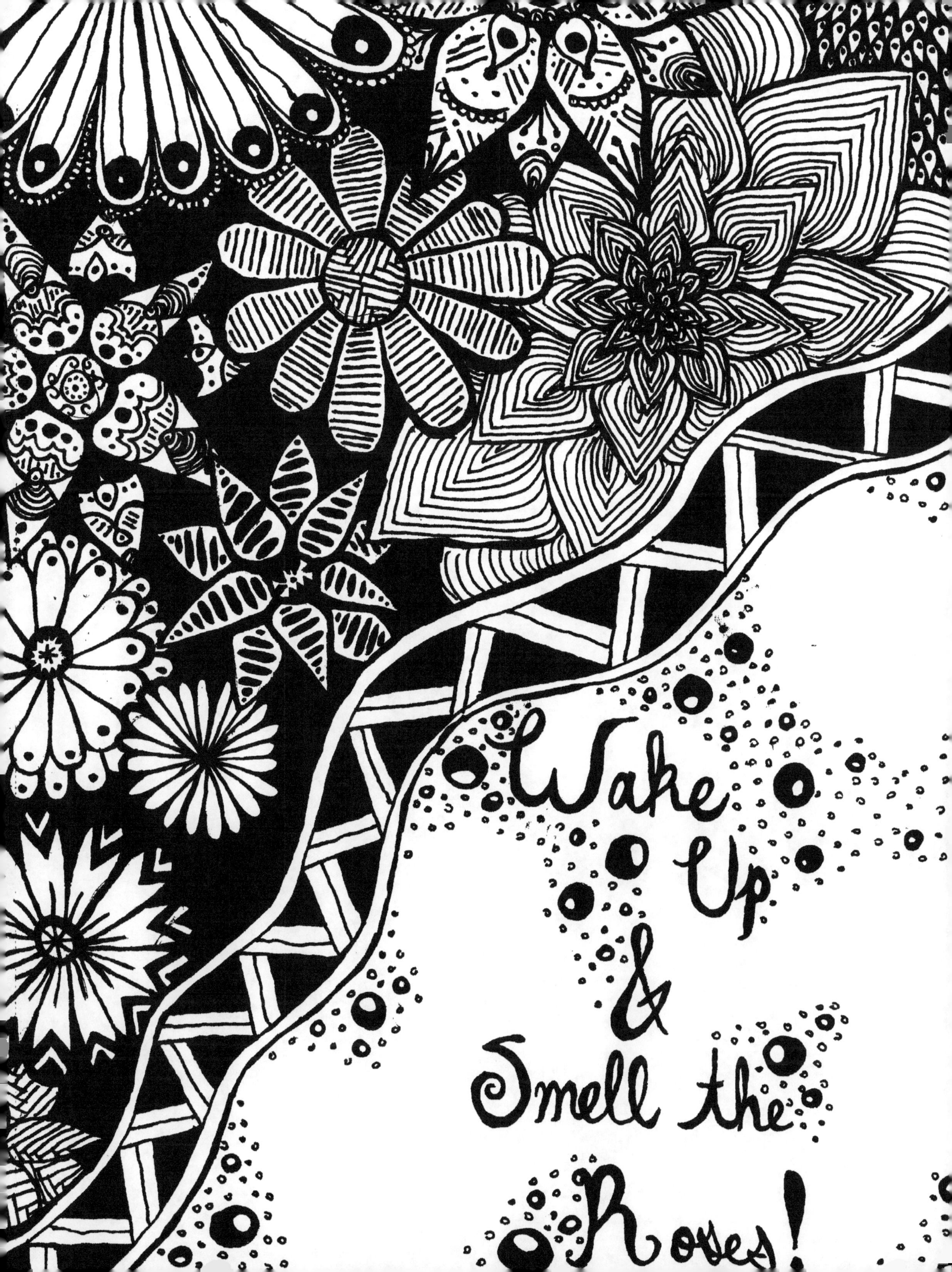
Wake Up
&
Smell the
Roses!

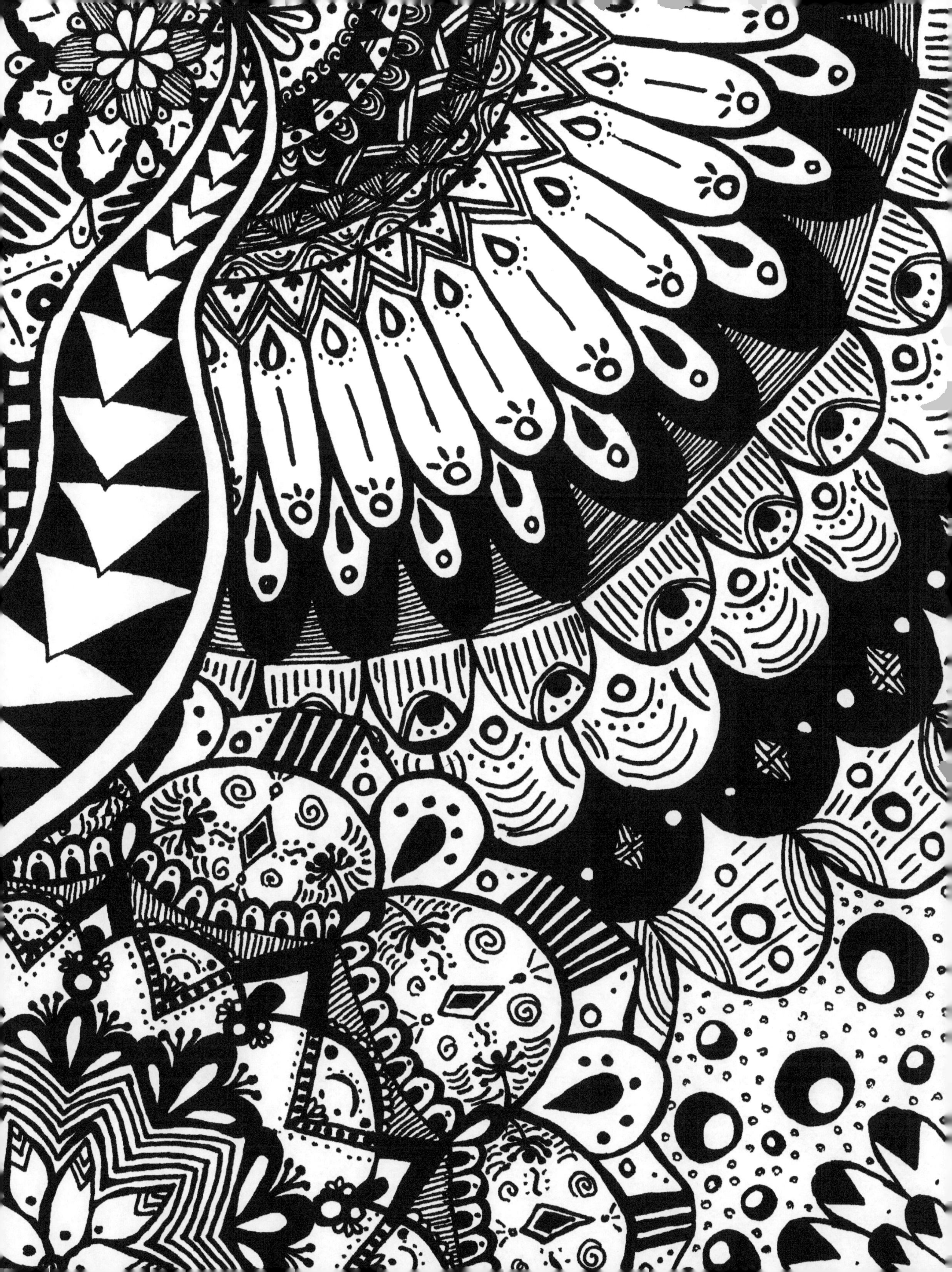

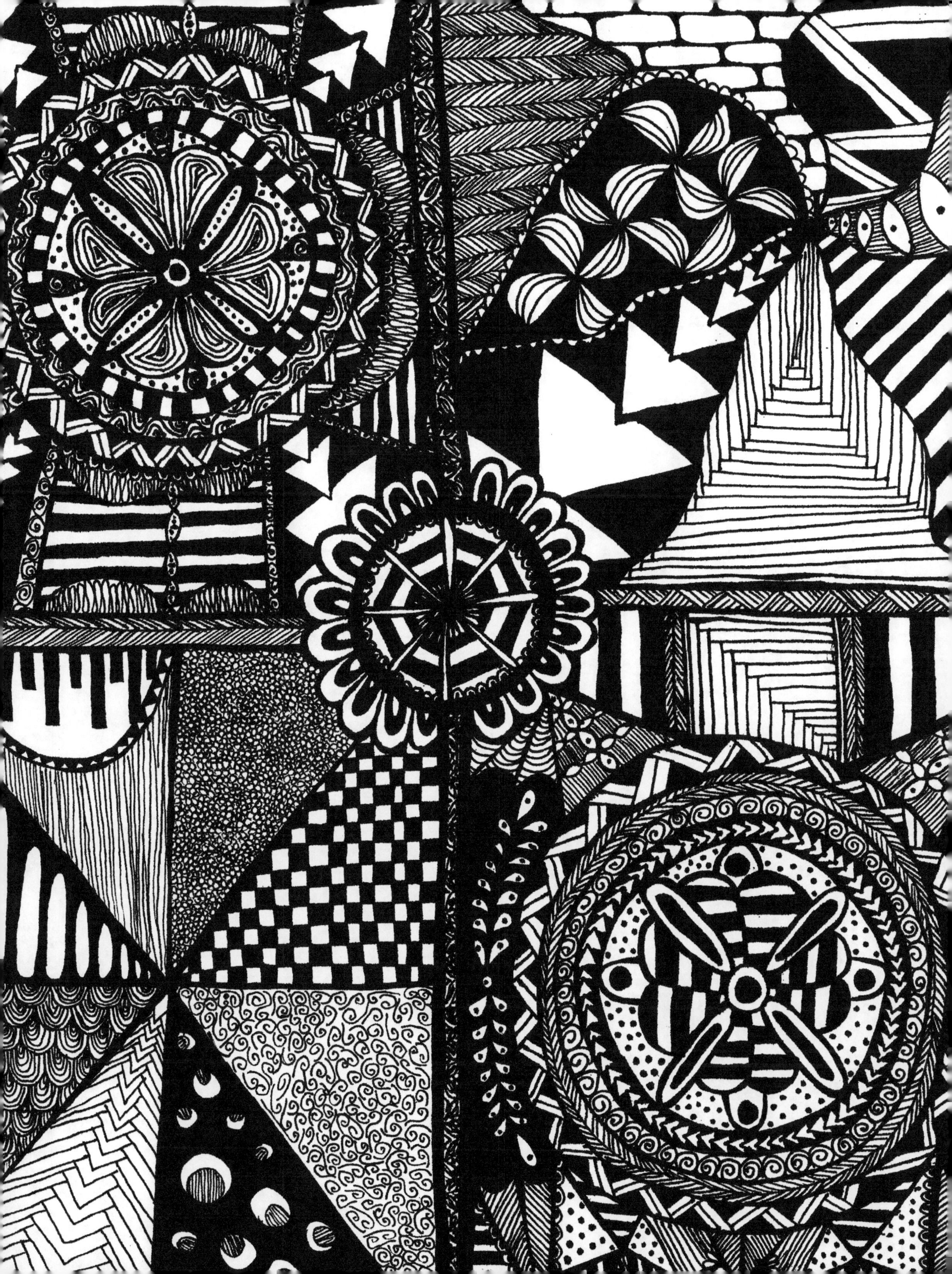

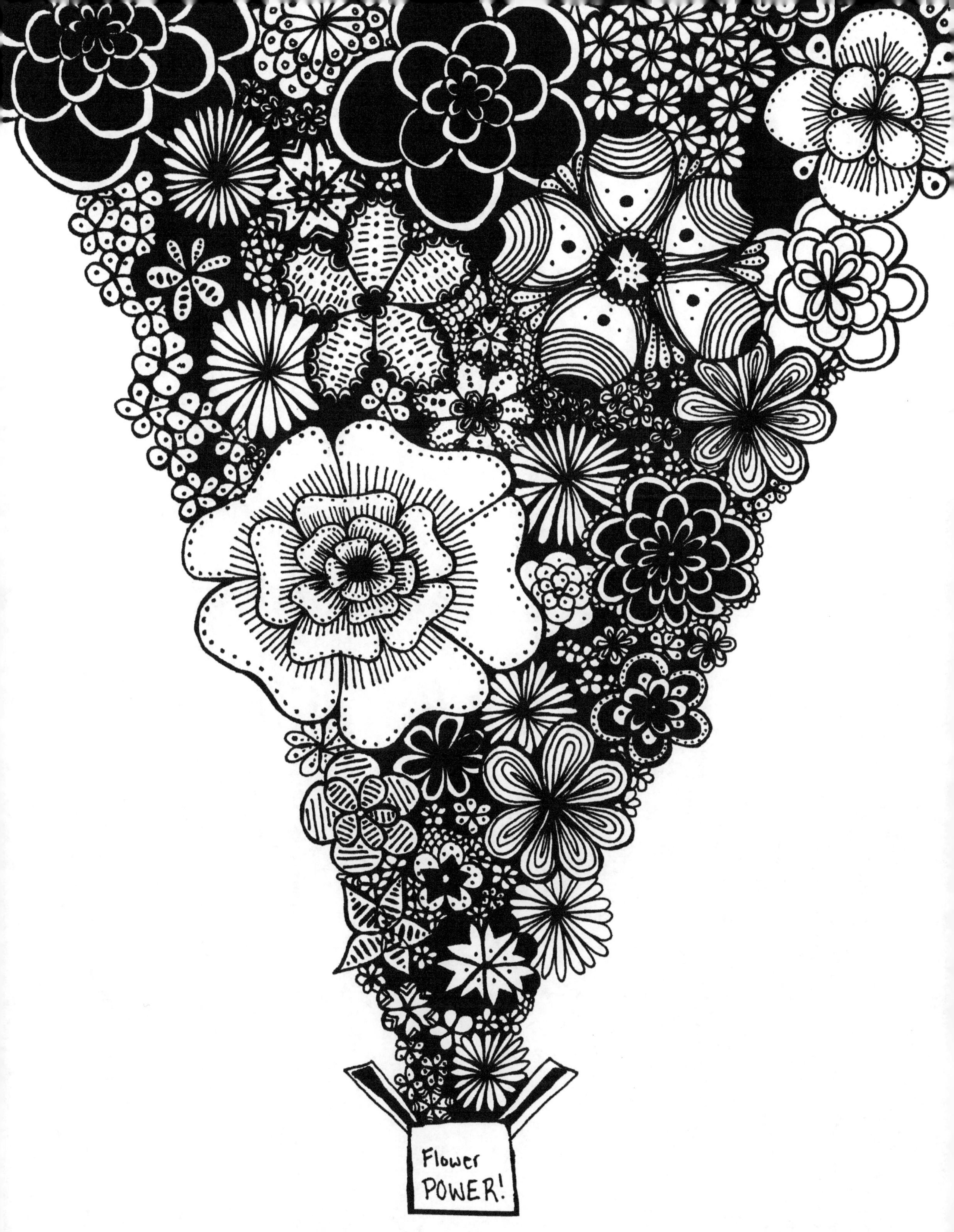
Flower
POWER!

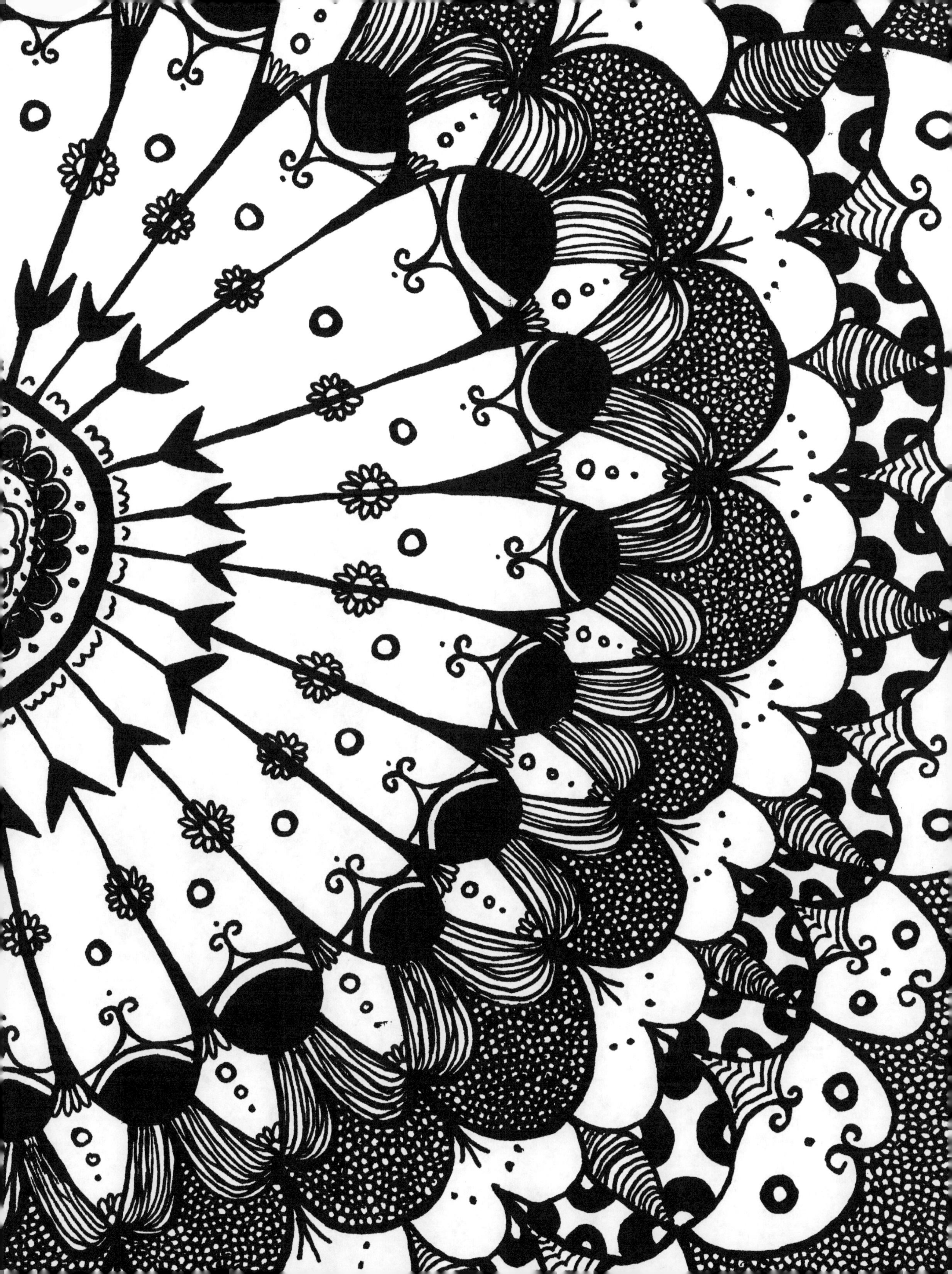

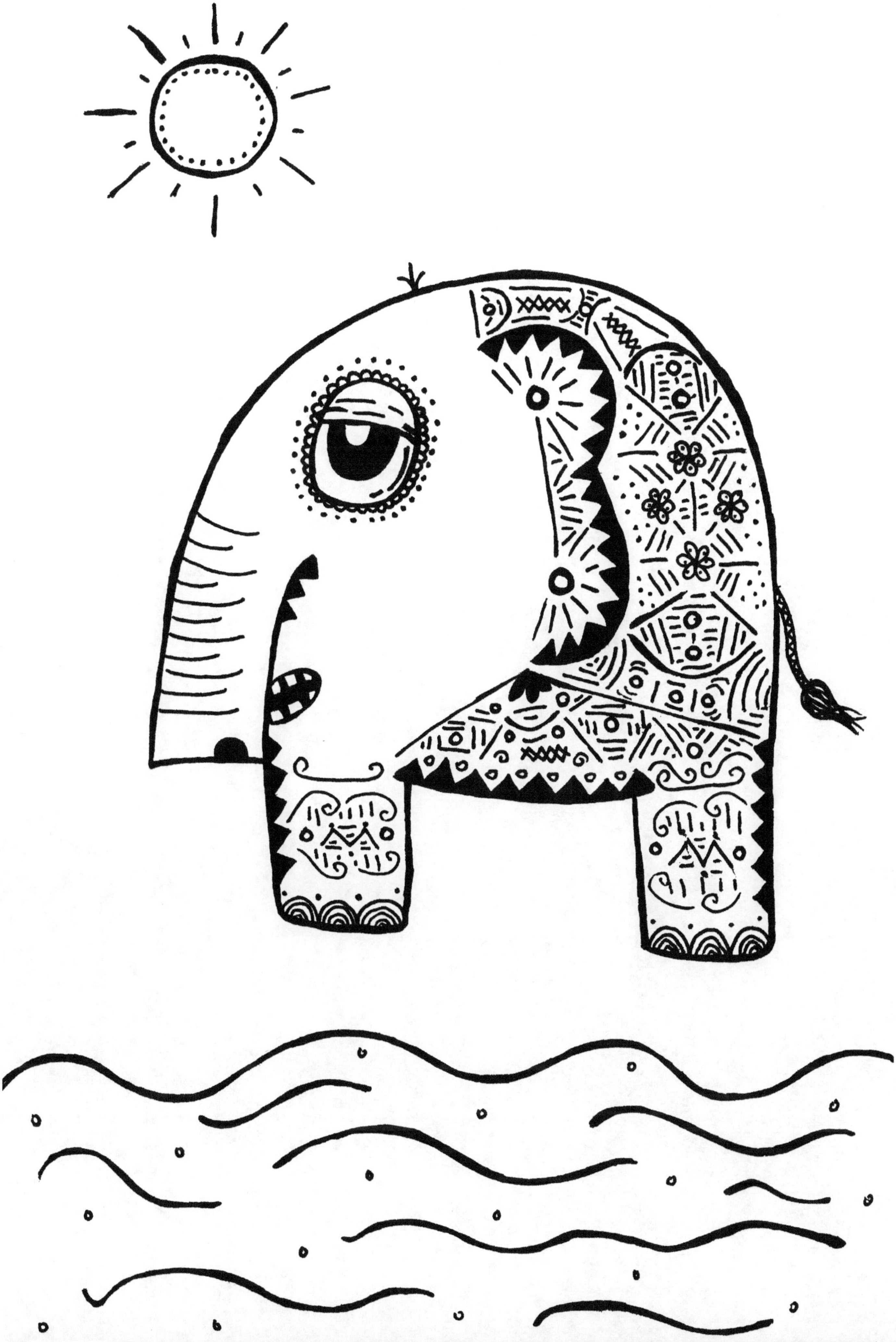

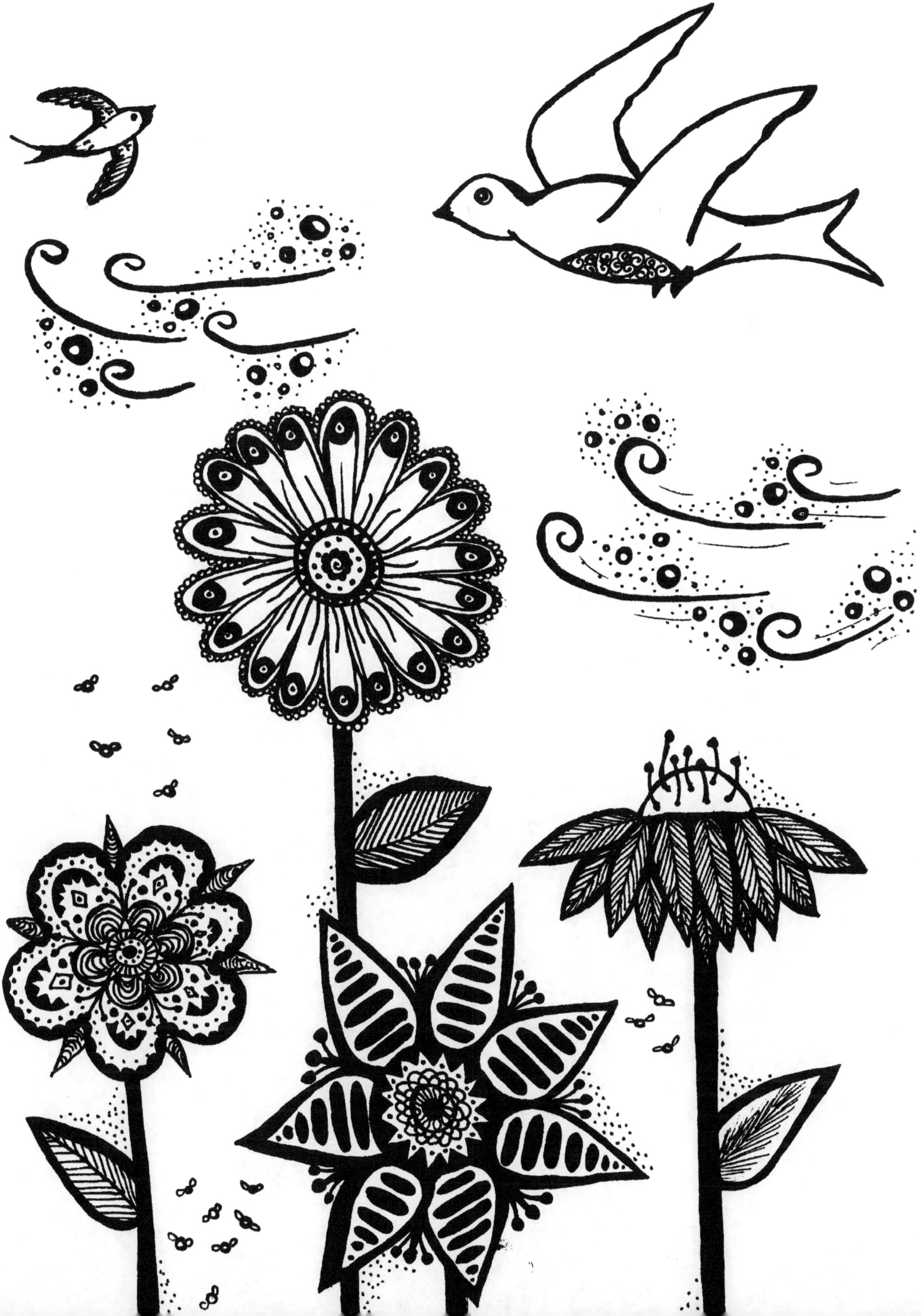

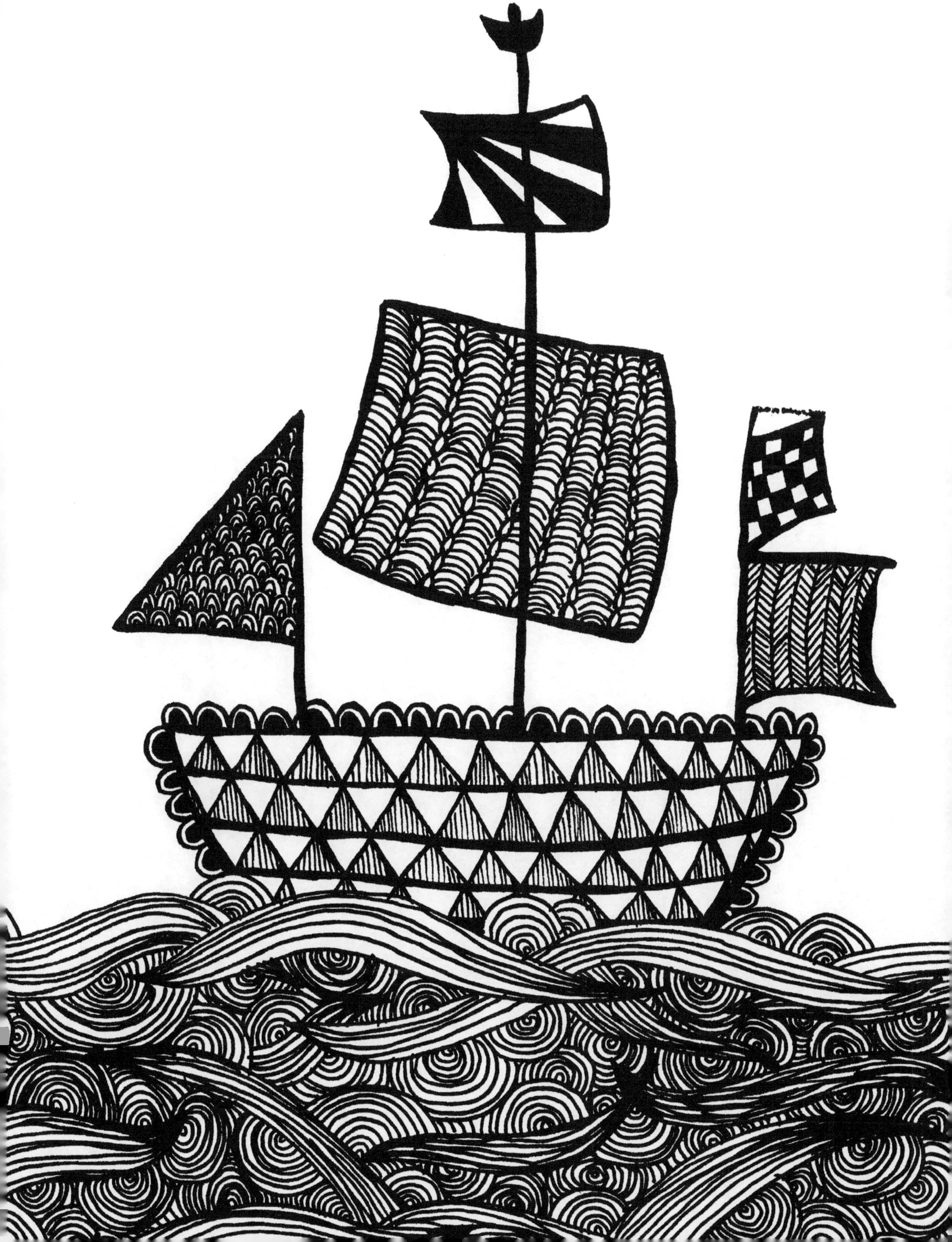

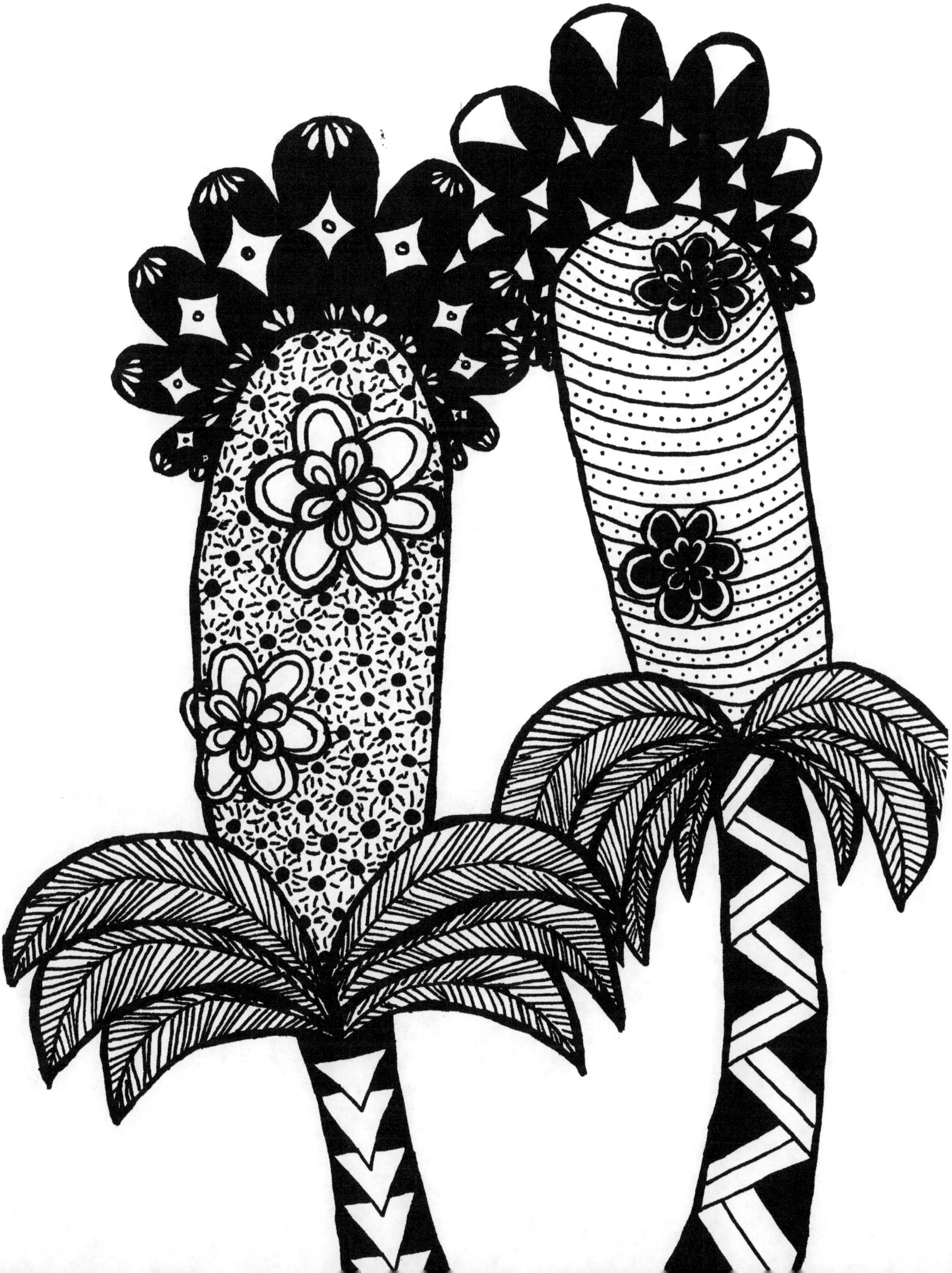

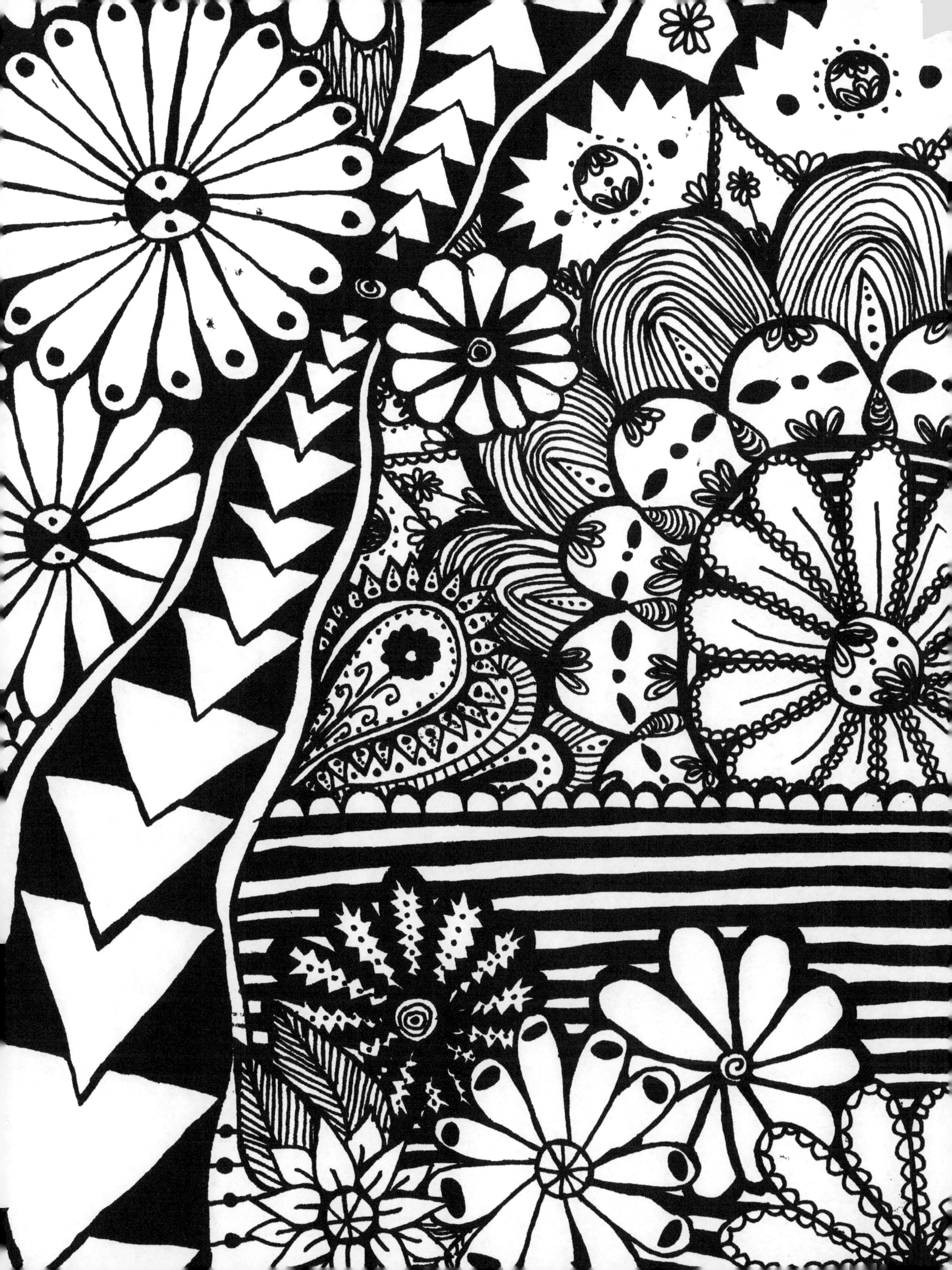

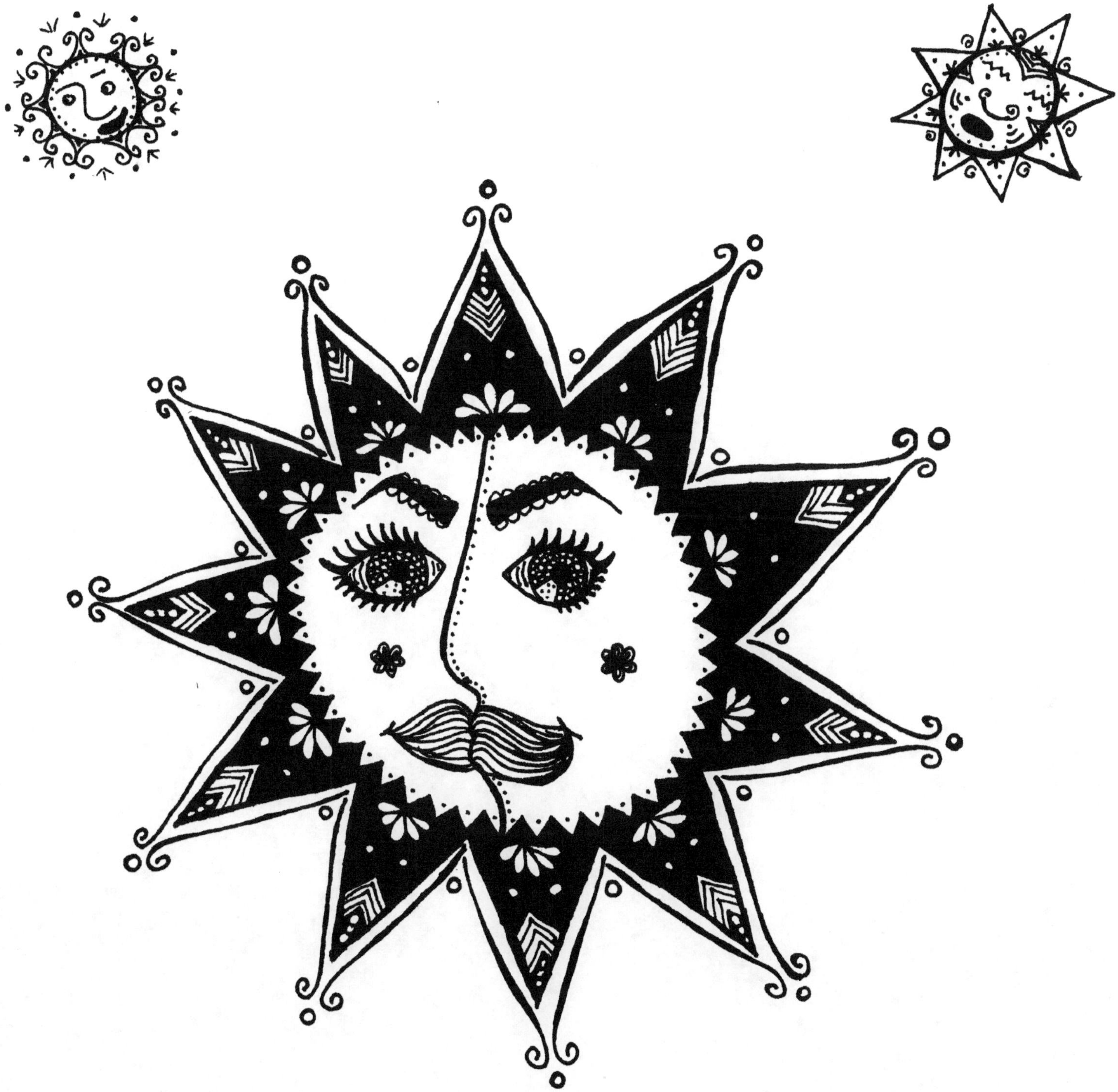

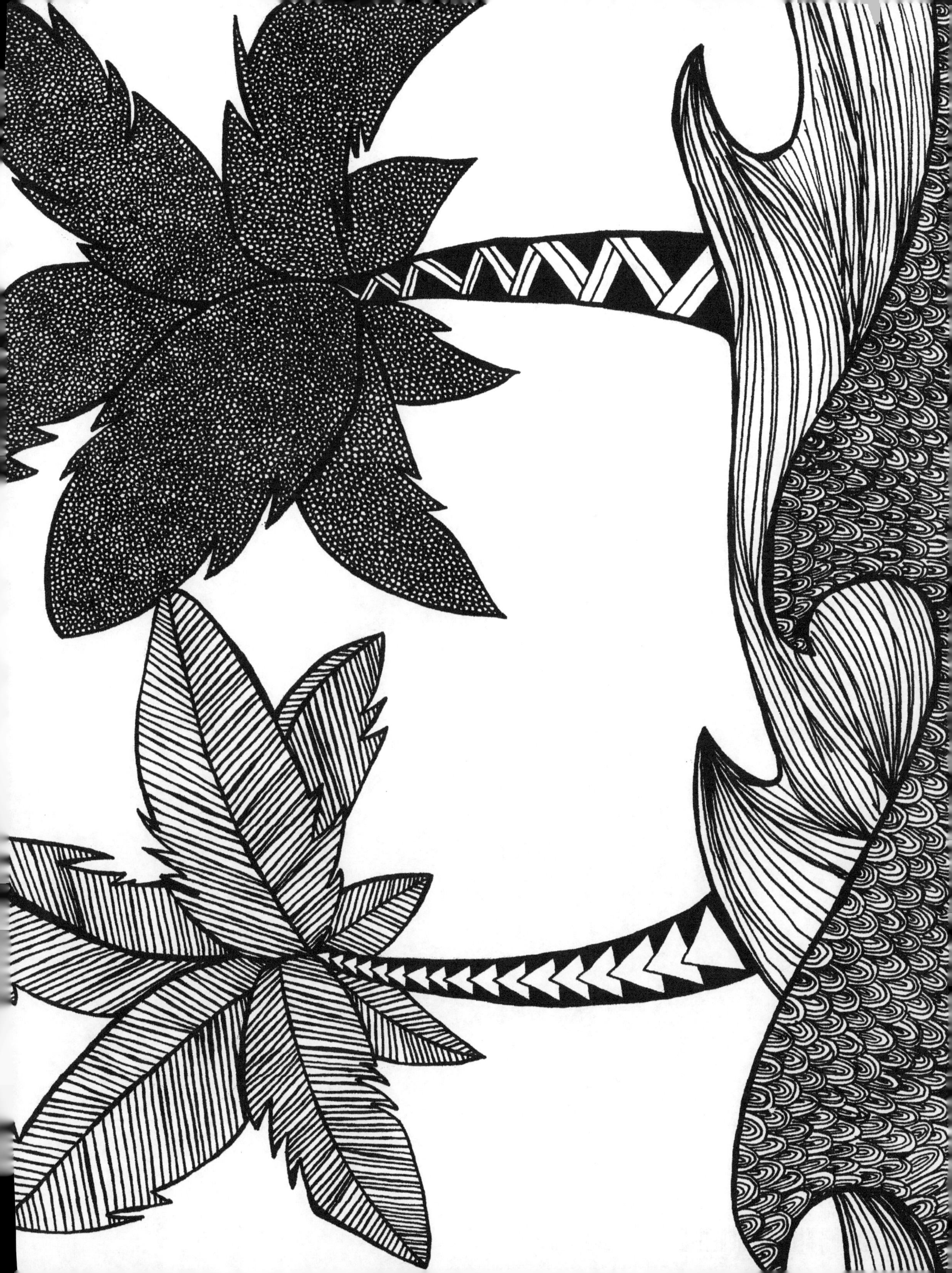

www.ingramcontent.com/pod-product-compliance
Lightning Source LLC
Chambersburg PA
CBHW080716190526
45169CB00006B/2396
9781523863013